# Kindred Trinity

David Nelson Bradsher
David Lee Caudill
Lorraine R. Sautner

Published by TJMF Publishing

Authors
David Nelson Bradsher
David Lee Caudill
Lorraine R. Sautner

Cover Design by Archer Graphics

Library of Congress Control Number: 2004112174
ISBN: 0-9759314-9-0

Printed in the United States of America
By Fidlar Doubleday of Michigan
December 2004

Three individuals, three localities, one dream.

We were brought together by a common love for the Art of poetry. As strangers, we shared a similar desire for spiritual serenity and tranquility, and through our words we found in each other what dwelled inside ourselves: love for family, for creativity, and an unmatched love for our Creator. In time, a bond grew and a beautiful kinship was created, sparking a fascination in what could only be described as a Kindred Trinity. We have come to care for each other, to rely on each other, and to love one other with an undying passion. We have become siblings not only in a benevolent sense, but in the spiritual sense we have long desired.

This could not have been possible without the help of some wonderful people along the way. We would like to thank our good friend Jim Furber and Emerging Poets for giving us the opportunity to be united, and for helping us to realize our dream of creating this book. To our families, thank you for standing by our sides through the good and the bad. We love you all so much. Thank you to Lord Byron, Edgar Allan Poe, Henry Wadsworth Longfellow, and Christina Rossetti for the inspiration and strength you have given us through your words. We would also like to express our faith and love for God. It was He who made us who we are, who brought us together, and who placed us in the loving families we are all so proud to be a part of. Thank you to all, and may God bless you.

David Nelson Bradsher
David Lee Caudill
Lorraine R. Sautner

# Kindred Trinity

vii

## David Nelson Bradsher

David Nelson Bradsher is a native and resident of Raleigh, North Carolina who only recently rediscovered the cathartic power of poetry.   By trade a partner in Bradsher and Bunn Insurance Agency, Inc., he is a 1989 graduate of the University of North Carolina-Chapel Hill with a B.A. in English.

David prefers to write in a more traditional verse than what is popular in today's society, drawing on influences from the Romantic Era such as Byron and Shelley.   He hopes to strike a chord with the readers by writing poetry that all can identify with and draw hope from.

He'd like to thank all at Emerging Poets; Lorraine Sautner and Dave Caudill (the other two members of the Kindred Trinity); and his family and his friends, without whom this would never have been possible.

# The Weathered Tome (A Night with Ghosts)

## I

One evenfall, I sat and browsed
The pages of a weathered tome.
'Midst glowing words from muses roused
My restless mind arose to roam.

## II

Imbibing friends expected me,
But Byron pried my thoughts from time.
Once steeped in Don Juan's poetry,
I sailed a sea of rolling rhyme.

## III

Then Shelley showed me Alastor,
The spirit of sheer solitude.
He ushered me through days of yore
Suggesting works I might include.

## IV

Then, Lo! I spied the clock and saw
The longer hand had spiked the six,
But magic and inspiring awe
Dissolved my plans to meet and mix.

## V

Enwrapped within archaic verse
With "thee" and "thou" and sundry words,
I delved in Coleridge to immerse
Myself in tales of sacred birds.

VI

From Keats, the best of Grecian urns,
Was praised by ode and topped my list,
And then the Scottish Robert Burns
Sang songs of lovely lasses kissed.

VII

When Tiger eyes were burning bright
The ghost of Blake was in the room,
And drafts of chill impaled the night
As Poe drew forth the Raven's gloom.

VIII

I wandered lonely as a cloud
With Wordsworth 'midst the daffodils,
And whilst we walked he mused aloud
Of beauty o'er the vales and hills.

IX

The Valkyries, with Thomas Gray,
Were Sisters at their busy loom.
From Hell, they spun a crimson day,
And stained the fields with mortal doom.

X

For mastery, the choice was clear,
As Shakespeare's sonnets touched the heart.
I shed a tear, and pleased my ear,
Whilst reading pure iambic art.

XI

Aurora's beam was glancing through
My window as I shut the book.
Outside, I glimpsed the sparkling dew,
White crystals on an em'rald brook.

XII

The fragrance of a new spring dawn
Was wafting in the morning air.
I padded through the glist'ning lawn
As whisp'ring breezes teased my hair.

XIII

The waking world seemed fresh and new,
Alive with April's pastel kiss.
I languished 'neath a dome of blue
And marveled at perfection's bliss.

XIV

The shadows of the lonely night
Will crawl inside me nevermore.
Now darkness quails in Muse's light
And thus avoids my open door.

XV

These pages, slight as onion skin,
Hold wisdom of a timeless kind.
So come, and let us now begin
To snap the choking ties that bind.

## XVI

True freedom comes to those who try
To brook the hosts of foolish pride.
Poetic souls refuse to die
When fueled to burn a fire inside.

Come Back To Me

O! night breeze, whisper low your lover's song,
A lullaby of moans that softly sing.
Emotion's rhythms pulse all summer long
Beneath the silver shine of moonlight's ring.
Romantic bliss reverbs, so pure and sweet,
Within our sandy bed, in cloistered dark.
The crashing waves keep time, a rolling beat,
Ere morning's silent rise, an amber arc.
But vengeful dawn is near, and wants the sky
To end for now our precious rendezvous.
'Til night's return we'll part in kissed goodbye
Beside the ebon swirl, reborn in blue.

When stars emerge and gleam upon the sea,
Immerse yourself in dark; come back to me.

True To Heart

'Midst plumes of smoke I float above
A pyre that my emotions fed.
The mercury of bleeding love
Embalms the heart I left for dead.

Untended wounds asphyxiate
The innocent, who trust too much,
And what prevents your hope's abate
When nothing's left for you to clutch?

The flame of wrath will heat the soul
When love departs and leaves you cold,
But anger ousts all self-control
With rage too hot for tongues to hold.

Defend against angelic thieves
Whose words are sweet but curdle soon.
Rebuke the lines a fool believes
When whispered 'neath a liar's moon.

A heart will break in careless hands
When sentiments turn hard and stale.
The injured victim understands
Too late that forcing love will fail.

Beware the thirsty parasites
Who claim to give, yet take away,
Extracting life from leeching bites,
They pledge to save, but mean to slay.

I've read, "To thine own self be true,"
And comprehend the Bard's intent.
The captain of your heart is you
And only fails with your consent.

Through Shakespeare's words I realize,
Polonius shares grand advice.
Believe your heart and not your eyes;
What happens once won't happen twice.

Half

I will traverse this wretched earth alone
In search of perfect love once mine, but lost;
Enlisting power forged in flesh and bone,
Expending soul no matter what the cost.
I feel her fingers tracing down my face,
Her silken voice still trickling through my mind;
Alas, her image burns through time and space,
Though wounded hope is limping far behind.
I'd found in her the better half of me,
And separation leaves me incomplete;
But here inside, I neither hear nor see
Surrender of my hope, nor love's defeat.

Still burning red within my aching heart
Remains the pulsing point of Cupid's dart.

Uncommon (Burial) Ground

As earth absorbs the gift of blood
And sips the salt of battle sweat,
The vanquished sink in tombs of mud
In sacrifice to freedom's debt.

The dying fade to agony,
For glory promised so much more.
A siege by land, or air, or sea
Sustains and feeds a hungry war.

This misery transcends all lines
Of creed or nationality,
For bullets, blades, grenades and mines
Are shrapnel of reality.

From Ilion to Normandy,
The clashes echo through the years.
The reaper swings his scythe with glee
And brings the rain of mourning tears.

Regardless of opinions formed,
By doves of peace or hawks of war,
Once blood imbues the beaches stormed,
All voices die amidst the roar.

So, let us meet on common grounds,
For in this place we all agree.
The men that lie beneath these mounds
Just gave their lives for you and me.

Covered Bridge (Gateway to Destiny)

Canto I

A covered bridge enshrouds the road
That crosses o'er to destiny.
Its shell is cracked; its boards are bowed,
Yet, still it stands and waits for me.
'Midst younger days, I saw this place,
Ere decades scrubbed its painted face.

My recollections of this bridge
Are not of wayward journeys through.
I'd gaze upon the distant ridge
And then resume the path I knew.
My rage would thwart attempts at change
That deigned to stretch my comfort's range.

I ventured out, but ne'er went far,
For trepidation held me back.
I sought, in vain, a guiding star,
But moonglow died in skies of black.
My only choice, I realized,
Embraced the change that I despised.

I set out on the usual road,
Well-trodden by familiar feet,
But 'neath my oft-increasing load,
I stumbled off the path I beat.
Unknown by most, and undefiled,
I lost myself within the wild.

Canto II

The way seemed shut, yet still I'd forge,
Besieged by beasts of dread and fear.
Past rustic miles I spied the gorge,
And sensed the clearing must be near.
I fought my way through tangled wood
To stand again where once I stood.

Before me yawns the deep ravine
That gapes below the bridge of fate.
To pen this act's unfinished scene
Would mean to brave the tunneled gate.
It beckons me to breach the door
By creeping 'cross the buckling floor.

Decisions loom that must be made
To map the course for coming days.
To take this path I once delayed
Would sever routes to other ways.
Beset by choices facing me,
My mind debates 'til thoughts agree.

'Tis best to find what time will hold,
Submitting to the whim of fate.
Most tales of lives that go untold
Grow stagnant whilst we hesitate.
But I, for one, must wait no more
To scribe my own immortal lore.

Canto III

The bridge is old, yet sits unused,
For never has its length been crossed.
Of self-neglect, I'm self-accused,
O'er weeks and months and years I lost.
Inaction is a trite defense,
And now I wish to recompense.

The penance I'm prepared to pay,
In minutes shall be satisfied.
My bitter guilt will drift away
On breezes from the other side.
I thrust myself into the dark
Determined now to make my mark.

Inside the bridge, the light grows dim,
But narrow slits let in the sun.
The golden beams, though spaced and slim,
Are beacons through this hollow run.
A ray of light is all one needs
To brook the gloom when darkness bleeds.

The rotting boards beneath my feet
Exhale with creaks of misery.
A splintered floor ensures defeat
For everything I strive to be.
I move ahead, and ne'er look back,
As fools retreat, the wise attack.

Canto IV

With cautious steps, the pace is slow,
And morning fades to afternoon.
Soon evening's weight will fall below,
To crush the sun and lift the moon.
The slivered shafts that aid my sight
Will vanish in the sea of night.

The bridge, though brief in measured length,
Seems endless on a passage through,
But those possessing inner strength,
At tunnel's end will earn their due.
Determination is my guide
When nocturne drowns the light inside.

Though sightless, still I ramble on,
For through the dark, the path runs straight.
The fear I'd known is nearly gone,
And soon I'll reach the virgin gate.
So far behind, from whence I came,
I hear the demons curse my name.

Pursuing me to no avail,
With careless speed they swiftly chase.
In bleaker days my heart would quail,
But now I lead this mortal race.
Their cries of hate and agony
Shan't sway the man I choose to be.

Canto V

The morning light will glimmer soon
And cast a glowing, amber smile.
I'll feel the warmth of early June
And then complete the golden mile.
I see the end not far away
Illumed within a brighter day.

The echoes of a shameful past
Are fading into memory.
The life I craved is here at last
And leaves the future up to me.
I'll stand upon uncharted earth
And usher in my soul's rebirth.

With lighter heart and faith restored,
The wooden planks no longer bend.
O'er every step and every board,
My wounds and scars begin to mend.
With quickened pace, in leaps and bounds,
My freedom's joyful song resounds.

I sprint into the dawning glow,
Emerging from the shadowed road.
The answers sought, at last I know,
For bravery has cracked the code.
I walk into a life anew,
Then turn to see what I've come through.

Canto VI

The fateful span that led me here
Shows clearly to the other ridge.
The path I walked in dread and fear
Is just a simple covered bridge.
Where darkness dwelt, the light now gleams
Within the gateway of my dreams.

The memories of the world I left
Have ceased to haunt my heart or head.
Their power stripped; they stand bereft,
And waste away if never fed.
I realize while gazing 'cross,
I've shed my skin, but bear no loss.

I hear the bridge begin to crack,
And, with a groan, the walls implode.
The shell that cloaked my path in black
Collapses on the wooden road.
Then, crumbling with a fractured roar,
The bridge falls to the canyon floor.

The gateway to the past is gone,
But isn't that a better thing?
'Tis time to move and ramble on,
And see what future days may bring.
I turn away and forge ahead,
For life moves on; the past is dead.

A Poet's Prayer

O'er endless miles that span this spinning earth,
Poetic minds reside in ev'ry place.
Unbridled joy upon a poem's birth
Is always shared, though seldom face to face.
Each heart exudes a passion, hot or cold,
Of subjects near and dear, or far and wide.
Though penned emotions ne'er will earn us gold,
We scribe our bleeding words with bursting pride.
Behold the benefits of distant friends,
For kindred souls are gems so rarely found.
We crave a reader with a mind that bends
In leiu of those whose thoughts are starched and bound.

Lo! Gather all who love the written arts
And pump creative blood to open hearts.

## The Red Dawn

Strange portents stain this naked dawn
That glowers down with red-rimmed eyes.
Once nocturne's raven wall is gone,
My spirit melts 'neath blazing skies.
Bad tidings coat the morning's rise
And slather me with sickly dread,
For day uncovers all the lies
Immersed in dust beneath my bed
Like grey remains of ancient dead.

O! let the night reclaim the earth
And shield me from the wretched day.
I rue the dawn's explosive birth
That stabs me with its searing ray.
Bright Helios, I wish to slay
With frost-tipped swords your burning heart.
I'd steal your glowing fire away
And give the night a quicker start
To brush the earth with onyx art.

In starless black, my pain recedes,
For there I shrink from human view.
My wounds could mend by kindly deeds,
But kindly deeds are sparse and few.
The innocence that I once knew
Is poured from me in scarlet flow,
Then mixed with morning's crystal dew
To give the day a crimson glow,
Creating sunrise from my woe.

The Invitation

An invitation came today,
Engraved in black calligraphy.
At six o'clock, the sixth of May,
My fading dreams will cease to be.
Your vows to him, espoused through tears,
Shall blur my eyes and burn my ears.

The moment of your sealing kiss
Shall dim the stars that light my eyes;
And, from the depths of my abyss
I'll claw at walls 'neath blackened skies.
The distance closed 'tween meeting lips
Enwraps my world in full eclipse.

You'll walk together down the aisle
With arms entwined as man and wife,
And look through me with radiant smile
Whilst striding by to leave my life.
The music of finality
Cues my bereaving malady.

I'll leave the church and you behind
Along with future plans I made;
And somewhere in my bitter mind
I'll start another masquerade.
Outside, I'll bow and wish you well;
Inside, I'll dig a deeper cell.

Requiescat In Pace

I walk above the ones who came before,
Among the markers of decaying stone.
O'er bridges 'twixt the dead and heaven's door,
The fallen lie together, yet alone.
Departing ghosts will ride the midnight mist,
On silver waves of fog, they roil and writhe.
Each name, in black, upon the Reaper's list
Has borne the hewing of his glinting scythe.
But dread not death, nor fear its minion's swing;
For peace awaits you on the other side.
The Father's light will sooth the bitter sting
And aid the spirit in its final glide.

Reunion's warmth at Glory's gleaming gate
Will melt the sorrow felt at life's abate.

Spring Of Hope

In pink-faced days of youth I ran
Through fragrant meadows all around.
But now you view a haggard man
Who trudges slow, and duty-bound.

The years escape in slimy night,
No clutching hands can grip their tail.
The vapors from their speeding flight
Descend upon me like a veil.

Three years ago, as life crashed down,
It buried me in winter gloom.
I lie beneath depression's gown
Within the cloister of my room.

For solitude, my only peace,
Is but a brief and sweet reprieve.
I've signed in blood a moral lease,
So ev'ry dawn I rise and leave.

My father's health is fading fast;
I labor 'neath an awkward cross.
The years of simple life have passed,
And taunt me with impending loss.

Potential wives are shunned in haste,
As time allows no social bliss.
My lips still crave the tingling taste
And sparkle of a lover's kiss.

## Sonnet To A Serpent

I shan't accept the false apology
That slides with slime and lies from serpent tongue.
The dark deceit of thine psychology
Infects the hearts in range of words hard-slung.
Thy foul injection spikes the purest souls
With poison spat that knows no antidote.
Through channels cleared with verbal puncture holes
The venom crawls into the victim's throat.
Alas! the malady is swiftly spread,
As one by one, the sick, forever stained,
Distribute death in droves 'til all lie dead
From mouths infected by the unrestrained.
Unfork thy tongue ere stabbing souls to gird
For kingdoms crumble 'pon a single word.

# The Bane Of Icarus

From Minos' tower, we took flight,
And fled the stone facade of grey.
On wax-dipped feathered wings so light,
We left the maze ere coming day.

For Daedalus, of hardy mind,
Would stare upon the churning sea.
He conjured means to quickly find
A way to soar, unchecked and free.

We flew away from Minos' wrath,
Towards the rising amber ring.
Through billowed puffs of father's path,
Was Helios, dawn's rising King.

His beauty called; I changed my course,
Against advice from father's voice.
Consumed and bent upon His force,
In youthful thrall, I made a choice.

Compulsion forced a foolish turn,
To yellow rays of greedy grasp.
Anointed by His sudden burn,
I flared amidst my painful gasp.

Ensnared by light, I failed to feel
The hungry flames of His desire.
My wings were burned in crawling peel
To withered ash, by dancing fire.

Bereft of wings, my body fell,
A comet spat from ruthless skies.
From Heaven's gate, I dropped to Hell,
A victim of His sizzling lies.

The sea became a frothing grave
Accepting me as sacrifice.
To depthless dark, the King then gave
A victim of ambitious vice.

The ocean closed and swallowed me,
Embalmed alone in shadowed murk.
A soulless corpse, no longer free,
Entombed below, where monsters lurk.

I washed ashore on unknown land
And laid to rest beneath His eye.
A shallow tomb of rock and sand
Restrained the man who tried to fly.

A price was paid for futile reach,
A lesson learned in fiery death.
Ambition spurs your judgment's breach,
And robs you of your living breath.

Diatribe In The Aftermath

A growling sky, with purple glare,
Unleashes rage from phantom wings.
Its wrath is charged with lightning's flare,
Cyclonic strikes, and sizzling stings.
Tornadoes, bane of new-born springs,
Will hibernate through wintry days,
Anticipating season swings
When flowers bloom 'neath golden rays,
Amidst the powdered pollen haze.

Pure beauty dawns in April's bloom,
But storms display unfettered might.
Congested clouds will cough their gloom
From tempest jaws that snap and bite.
A messenger devouring light
Reminds the world how small we are,
As brief eclipses bring the night
'Til bested by the brightest star,
The Sun, protecting from afar.

As Nature ends her roaring fit,
Sad eyes survey the aftermath.
The lamp of day has been relit
Exposing what befell her path.
The targets of her temper's wrath
Hold memories that never wane,
For Nature is a psychopath
Whose laughter falls 'midst stinging rain,
Within a howling hurricane.

## Progression

The spiring stalagmites of splintered dreams
Adorn my damaged mind like littered waste.
Their jagged shards have dammed melodic streams
Of rhythmic thoughts that danced with fluid haste.
My placid mood has roughly been replaced
And stands aggrieved, besieged with fire and ice,
The glaring elements I bravely faced
When simple words no longer would suffice
To save my failing grip on fleeting paradise.

In my internal wars, at last I've learned
The victor matters not in such a fight;
For once the dead are piled on pyres and burned
Both sides are left remorseful and contrite.
When fiery battlements are glowing bright
Inside the swirling chaos of my mind,
I'm blinded by the mix of smoke and light,
And mournful of the dreams I leave behind,
For havoc reigns when self-esteem is undermined.

Without a hero, I'll believe in me
To right the wrongs within that I allowed;
I'll lead myself through insecurity,
Emerging from the inner war unbowed.
The pungent smoke will fade, and I'll stand proud,
Aware the key that I alone possess
Will open wide the gifts that God endowed:
Redemption from the scourge of self-distress,
Enacted by the fears I never would address.

Eternal Isle

Alone, I wander down the beach,
Along the shores of Emerald Isle.
A ship sails near, yet out of reach,
"Like her," I think, and force a smile.

My eyes reflect the rolling sea
With rage that clouds the deepest blue;
Not rage at "her," but rage at me,
For passing by the love I knew.

When I say "her," I should say "them,"
For time and time, this tale repeats.
All thoughts of love, I self-condemn,
Then execute my own defeats.

My wistful smile is upside down,
Reversed by my dyslexic soul;
Though I may grin, inside I frown,
For deep within, I've lost control.

'Tis easier to wear this mask
Than show you how I really feel.
Impossible, a lover's task,
To warm a heart that's wrapped in steel.

I've written of my fortress walls,
The place where I exist alone.
I pray to God the castle falls,
But I'm the one who stacked the stone.

As Emerald Isle succumbs to night,
I strain to gaze across the sea.
The ship has glided out of sight,
But not as far as love from me.

Battle's Dawn

Aurora kissed mine eyes this gentle morn,
Her golden lips upon a sleep-stilled face.
Another day conceived in night, and born,
Will shine with fledgling light and charming grace.
Soft music of the dawn will coat our ears
And quell the demons of nocturnal wrong.
Arise at once and cast away thy fears,
For battle's crash awaits the brave and strong.
Though comrades fall amidst the fog of war,
Unleash your wrath upon our reckless foe.
Their hearts will quail beneath our charging roar
On fields of flowers where the daisies grow.

Enjoy the tranquil peace of fragrant dawn,
For soon the horn will blow, and beauty's gone.

Arbor Magic

Amidst the swaying trees we stroll
On shadowed roads that lie in grey.
A deeper path leads to the soul
Of ancient woods at shut of day.

The waning glow succumbs to night,
And cloaks us in the ebon earth.
Our kindred minds, bereft of sight,
Release our passion's bright rebirth.

In blind emotion, yielding trust,
Our pulsing need now leads the way.
A sultry mix of love and lust
Illumes the black like dawn's first ray.

In morning frost, I take your hand,
We leave beneath the arbor smile.
Two merged as one in wooded land,
To consummate the crowning mile.

Mining Mem'ries

The sentimental music plays
Within the web that spans my mind,
Imploring grainy yesterdays
To color mem'ries life designed.

The present scrolls in grey despair
And weights my heart with lead distress,
But can a soul enact repair
By finding methods to regress?

A childhood full of simpler times
Could give my mood the needed kick,
Though ditty songs and kiddie rhymes
Would lack the force for walls so thick.

I scan to early teenage years
To seek what adolescence lacked,
But acne scars and newfound fears
Combined as awkward change attacked.

The recollections of my youth,
Still hold for me a vivid joy,
Yet searching 'midst a deeper truth
Reveals a frightened, lonely boy.

Alas! the echoes of the past
Shan't sooth the pain I feel today.
My swirling skies are overcast
Like mem'ries filmed in dusty grey.

## Arlington

'Neath sacred sod lie crumbled dreams,
In hollow shells of parted souls.
Six feet of dirt shield echoed screams,
And elegies of tragic tolls.

The graveyard spans in green and grey,
With paths of glory winding through.
The hues of Independence Day,
Will burst in red, and white, and blue.

The ghost of Lee protects the field,
And those who earned Potomac peace.
On hostile ground, their fates were sealed,
But strength and honor never cease.

The endless lines of crosses glow,
In sun-shot rays of mourning's dawn.
Our heroes rest in ev'ry row,
And grace the lush Virginia lawn.

The living flame of JFK,
Ensures they'll never lie alone.
Their names are etched in silver-grey,
And pride preserves the marbled stone.

So, walk in silence, and reflect,
The sacrifice our soldiers made.
Their selfless acts deserve respect;
Our gratitude shall never fade.

Prelude To Dream

Encircled by the words I write,
Secure inside their seamless shell,
I scribble verse by Muse's light
And pen self-portraits set in Hell.

The ink of life is bled in black
Yet sleepless eyes are shot with red.
The clock ticks on but never back,
And who foresees what lies ahead?

The wisdom gleaned from harder years
Lies buried 'neath my bleary stare.
Exhuming long forgotten fears
Will leave a soul exposed and bare.

I write the truth behind my shield,
Anonymous in honest purge.
The flowing quill I daily wield
Unleashes my creative surge.

I settle in, revealing more,
And, slouching down, I slip away.
While digging through my shredded core,
I find I've nothing left to say.

My purge complete, I drop the pen,
Retiring to a well-earned rest.
I'll dream the dreams of pensive men
Since mind and body acquiesced.

Prisoner In The Tower

I float within an absinthe dream,
Outside the realm of placid sleep.
I crave the moon's enlightened beam,
But toss beneath the roiling deep.

My demons lurk and haunt the gate,
In leering masks of lovers lost.
Their sentiment imbrued by hate,
And cold seclusion bears the cost.

I stack these bricks on sleepless fears,
And bar the doors with self-control.
With mortar mixed in bitter tears,
I wall around my shrouded soul.

I gaze outside the turret's port,
And watch my life scroll quickly by.
I've viewed the pass of ev'ry sort,
Resisting change as seasons die.

I toil above, each day the same,
A captive in the tower's cone.
I yearn to play the living game,
Instead I sit and age alone.

# The Ides Of Autumn

My spirit rustles on the Ides of fall
'Midst swirling leaves that stir me from my sleep.
I shall arise renewed to heed the call
With lies to end, and promises to keep.
The trust I injured now shall be restored
With honor held above all qualities;
Another failure I can ne'er afford
When challenged by my mind's frivolities.
So serious the days of harder times,
As childhood toys are placed upon a shelf,
Forgotten in the shift to crisper climes
When man emerges from my boyish self.

The harbinger of change at summer's end
Is carried by the brisk October wind.

Chasing Byron

We scribble in iambic rhyme,
And emulate your classic verse;
Your living words have weathered time
And breathe beyond the mortal curse.

So use us, Byron, if you will,
To share your penned philosophy;
For those who know you love you still,
And what you are we burn to be.

Our greatest wish will ne'er come true,
To catch the muse that lit your mind;
Real genius stirred the heart in you
With greatness of the rarest kind.

Though death too soon stole you away,
Your art is worth a thousand lives;
Byronic heroes of today
Ensure your perfect work survives.

The links of this poetic chain
Hold strong despite one soul's demise;
Though moody, flawed and sometimes vain,
No weakness shall prevent our rise.

The Rattle Before The Strike

The swirling smoke from all your bridges burned
Invokes a putrid haze that chokes the air.
Your foolish "friends" are weak; the tide has turned,
And self-made enemies are everywhere.
Unworthy for this war that you declare,
If you disturb this nest: expect a sting.
You threw the gauntlet down, so now prepare,
To suffer for the trouble that you bring,
Which stokes a scalding fire within this king.

You hide in your disguise, but I see through
The humorous facade that you portray.
Adorned in red and green, and gold and blue,
Appearances deceive, but not this day.
I'll strip your spangled garb, and leave you grey,
Bereft of color, so that all may see,
The tragic joke within, on full display,
'Til your hypocrisy will cease to be,
And leaden skies will drip with your debris.

# Rural Reflections

The thunder's roar and pelting rain,
In tandem drum the rusty tin.
Percussion's crash is metal's pain
And raps a rhythmic rooftop din.

This crumpled house is old and scarred
By season's change and weather's blast,
Whilst weeds have sprouted in the yard
Like sentries grown to guard the past.

'Twixt Bushy Fork and Hurdle's Mill,
The remnants echo faded years.
Forgotten ghosts that time won't kill
Preserve what always disappears.

I walk a path of dirt and stone,
A muddy road to memories,
And though I journey all alone,
Fell voices drift upon the breeze.

Where crops had stood in green or gold
Lies lonely earth of endless span,
Yet still I picture days of old
When work begun ere dawn began.

These barns now ail in disrepair
And silently succumb to rot.
But, through my sentimental stare,
The mind retrieves what time forgot.

The images of yesteryear
Are dreams that thrive inside my head.
Though far away, they draw a tear,
With recollections of the dead.

And so I stand in pouring rain,
To soak in my lost innocence.
As years deliver loss and gain
Reflections form the best defense.

Death Of A Warrior Poet

Impaled upon a point of silver dread,
The bayonet had lanced, and entered clean.
My burning gut was gored, and quickly bled,
By gleaming steel 'neath dawn's illuming sheen.
At evenfall's approach, the time grows late,
And bears the dimming dark of my last day.
I know that consciousness will soon abate
And dwindling breath will cease here, as I lay.
Despite the pain of this, my final hour,
I find the inner peace to ponder life.
The Spring of youth was sweet, but love was sour,
And sharp regrets incise me, like the knife.

Upon this field, I die at twenty-two,
Amidst the thought, "I never said, 'I do'."

38

Raison D'Etre

True greatness comes from sacrifice,
Of those who strive and thus excel.
No selfishness or crippling vice
Prevents a hero's flight from Hell.

Though obstacles may litter roads,
Devouring light upon the path,
Adversity will pen the odes
That sing defeat of failure's wrath.

Determined to elude the scourge
That hews the hearts of quailing souls,
A poet will embrace the purge,
And journey far to conquer goals.

In darker days, hold fast to hope,
And let your quill imbue the weak.
Creative minds will scale the slope,
And stand atop the jagged peak.

By A Thread

Alas! O God, allow me peace;
Prevent my life from crumbling down;
Or, grant this soul its sweet release
In tides of tears, so I may drown.
My sanity or tragic death,
Please save me or reclaim my breath.

I clutch a frayed and burning rope,
So why am I still holding on?
I scream for light and grasp for hope,
But night just fell, and hope is gone.
Each second's tick is borrowed time,
And I cannot descend or climb.

By flame or weight, the rope will break,
And what then shall become of me?
Shall I endure each past mistake
In scenes unleashed by memory?
Am I to see where I went wrong,
Or hear my own bereaving song?

Parris Island

The endless sacrifice extends
Beyond the range of future view,
For ev'ry day my mission ends
Beneath the heavens' midnight blue.

But duty calls as morning dawns,
And beats the sun to rise and shine.
While silver dew adorns the lawns,
I stride amidst the fragrant pine.

I heed the rules of men of old,
With "Strength and Honor" as my creed,
And bring my brothers to the fold,
To multiply our thriving breed.

For youth must rise as elders wane,
To journey through this churning world.
My vigilance is evil's bane,
To storm the dark, a flag unfurled.

In wicked times, the good may quail,
But valiant hearts will still survive.
Though each of us may sometimes fail,
Our message shall remain alive.

Stalemate

A valiant pawn begins the match
Of selfish-versus-selfless me;
The goal: pursue and deftly catch
Components of my destiny.

A test of wit and skill ensues
'Twixt pieces on a checkered field;
But part of me is forced to lose
Before my will is thus revealed.

The thrust and parry, to and fro,
By pawn and bishop, rook and knight,
Will weave a ragged ebb and flow
Within the clash of black and white.

The black shall represent desire,
The things I crave but never need;
Enkindled from a darker fire,
Enabled by a reckless greed.

The white shall symbolize the heart
Of service and of sacrifice;
For virtue is a lonely art
When challenged by a tempting vice.

Both colors vie to capture kings
To claim the board and seize the day,
But my allegiance splits and swings
And shades my mind a neutral grey.

The Villain Inside

Proclaimed a fool by mirrored eyes,
They gleam with love and hate entwined.
The glass reflects the self-told lies
That forge a villain in my mind.

He takes away, but ne'er gives back,
And steals my will with smooth technique.
Then, camouflaged in nightmare black,
He plagues the pleasant dreams I seek.

Which role is mine within this game,
The hunter or the hunted prey?
Whenever I demand his name
He smirks at me and slips away.

I chase him through my whirring mind,
A dizzy maze of spinning wheels.
But footfalls close in right behind
And, lo, he's nipping at my heels.

The chase goes on within my soul,
A race without a finish line.
For madness has an endless goal
To first destroy, then redesign.

## The Passing Of The Poetic Torch

Unbidden fate awaits me now
Down roads of mist that I must follow.
The dreams I kept, I now endow
To you, my friend, for I am hollow.

Afford these dreams their due respect;
Here, take my pen; employ it well.
Look to the future, but reflect
On my mistakes that earned me Hell.

I take my leave without regret
Aware that you will bear the flame;
As one poetic son does set
Another waits to gain his fame.

'Neath blackened skies, the tides will turn,
But through it all, keep warm the spark.
The torch I pass lives whilst it burns,
A kindred candle in the dark.

Poetic Brothers

Poetic siblings heed their common muse,
And scribble burning thoughts on parchment skin.
Though able minds will harbor varied views,
Creative blood flows thick amongst these men.
A trinity of bards in rhythm's sway,
The common three invoke a draining purge.
Submerging deep in swirling seas of grey,
They drown their pulsing pain in salty surge.
But agony persists, though spilled in ink,
And fevered need emits a junkie's quake.
Bereft of art, their quailing hopes will sink,
So cramping fingers scrawl with peace at stake.

Their inky "fix", obtained through flowing arts,
Prevents the final fall of heavy hearts.

The One(S) That Got Away

Your sentiment holds greater worth
Than flailing souls are worthy of;
Instead, bequeath it to the earth
To shield from me your saving love.

'Tis better to avert my eyes
Than see the smile that I adore;
For when this passion fades and dies,
I'll look on sweetness nevermore.

In every case, I've done just this;
I've claimed a heart, and thrown it down,
'Til pearly dreams of wedded bliss
Are caked with mud and coated brown.

You see, my dear, what I've become?
A monster with a gentle face.
Your kiss feels dead, as I am numb,
Except for stabs of sharp disgrace.

Someday I'll want to find this spot
Where love was buried underground.
For now, however, love me not,
And leave my side without a sound.

I beg you please don't say goodbye,
Just turn your back and walk away.
I'll watch you go, then softly cry,
While wishing you would fight to stay.

## Of Dreams And Nightmares (The Staircase)

Deep clouds of mem'ry swab the mind
With antiseptic dreams in white,
For days of youth o'er time go blind
And only see in slumber's light.

The pathways to the realm of sleep
Are winding stairs embossed with gold,
But watch thy step, the rise is steep,
And drops to depths that nightmares hold.

By Heaven's glow, or flames of Hell,
The lamp of dreams is fueled and lit,
But which will spark, no one can tell,
'Til conscious and subconscious split.

When morning dawns, and bids thee "Wake!"
Thine eyes betray the night's results,
For dreams of dark and wicked make
Will redden eyes and race the pulse.

So, ere thou rest thy weary head
Lay down the weight of troubling strife.
The dreams of joy or heavy dread
Shall bleed inside thy wakeful life.

Parchment Catharsis

A swimming haze of random thought
Are misty dreams inside my head.
The words pursued and phrases caught
Are bared and scribed from feelings bred.

The pen performs a surgery,
Exsanguination of the mind.
Sheer honesty slays perjury,
And renders demons dumb and blind.

My freedom flows to bloodshot soul,
Reviving swift a heart grown cold.
An actor born to fill the role
Of Lazarus, with quill of gold.

I burn to write with earthquake words,
And burning immortality.
A shepherd leading human herds
Away from stark banality.

This southpaw heeds the rhythm's call,
Catharsis mixed with gauche and grace.
Emotions rise and tears will fall,
To make my mind a placid place.

## Self Cannibals

The cemetery plot of weak mankind
Lies deep and dark, but ne'er in dirt and stone.
The crimson life machine that God design'd
Is nestl'd 'neath a mesh of blood and bone.
Though rhythmic beats still thump, it's often known
Some hearts are sacrific'd for wicked goals.
A hungry greed attacks and eats its own
As thoughtless fools will chew away their souls,
Extinguishing all light within the holes.

The heartless pass their lives in scenes surreal,
Bereft of signs of true humanity.
They live and breathe the air, but never feel
While clawing through their blind insanity.
The ravag'd soul succumbs to vanity
And piece by piece, last vestiges erode
'Til nothing's left but spew'd profanity
To clot and dam the blood that freely flowed
And kill the waning soul that smil'd and glow'd.

The Jester

The Jester writhes in shadowed gloom,
'Til beckoned by the summons bell.
He leaves his barren, musty room,
A brief release from private hell.

He dons the painted mask of mirth,
A bright facade of trumped design.
This Harlequin of royal birth,
The fool within the Monarch's line.

He plays his part in multi-hue,
Atop the stage of starry light.
In green and yellow, red and blue,
His clothes distill the clotting night.

Exuding joy for all to see,
He buries drama far below.
By spreading warm, infectious glee,
He sets their crimson hearts aglow.

But far beneath the glamour shell,
A depthless pit awaits in black.
The wasted, hollow wishing well,
Will want the spangled Jester back.

Upon return of eventide,
All laughter dies along with day.
His charms are locked so deep inside,
The colors dim, and fade to grey.

## Gigas Dormiens

The seams that cross 'twixt heart and mind
Are sheer emotions bound by thread.
The mind is shrewd, the heart is blind,
But joined together, underfed.

The union holds, though tenuous,
For bubbling words erupt in haste.
A war, insane and strenuous,
Ensures the weak are laid to waste.

Destruction reigns o'er tepid souls
That lack internal fortitude.
For heat lives not in simmered coals,
But embers stoked by passion's mood.

The pressure mounts and stitches fray
Along the fissure's melting seams.
White doves of peace are blown away
By winds of wrath and piercing screams.

A sleeping giant, now awake,
Will rise against an ancient force.
The sky will bruise and Earth will shake,
Along his grim and ruthless course.

Too long he slept in wistful dream,
Immune to his environment.
His focused glare will fix its beam
Upon the target of his bent.

The shredded strings have pulled apart
To snap the bonds of his restraints.
A mind shan't douse a burning heart
With arguments, or harsh complaints.

He walks the path of destiny,
A darker journey wreathed in dread.
But still he forges, bold and free,
Along a road most fear to tread.

With ev'ry step, the giant grows,
And reaches up to dizzy height.
He towers o'er his quaking foes,
Who shrink beneath his daunting might.

They send a boy to sling a stone,
In hopes to claim the bitter game;
But in the end, he dies alone,
For Daevid is the giant's name.

Peace Amidst Chaos

A scrolling sky is painted sad,
And weeps in grey above my life.
I teeter past the edge of mad,
On balance beams of razored strife.

The years of seige have lanced my heart,
To kill the dreams of days now passed.
Combusting hopes have blown apart,
Expelling ashes from the blast.

The stench of Satan's scorching breath,
Now drips upon my straining neck.
A fool I'll be if snared by death,
A joker wild within its deck.

But now I've found the strength to win,
Despite the force of death's machine.
Above this life's despairing din,
I gather peace 'neath heaven's sheen.

## Substance

Oh, spare my eyes the glare of gold
That blinds the truth I burn to see;
My treasure is the quill I hold
With ink that bleeds, and sets me free.

With parchment, quill, and candlelight,
My Muse is all I shall require
To quell the tempest in my night
That mutes me 'mid its howling gyre.

The value of the written word
Is multiplied in needful times,
When masters from the grave are heard,
Immortalized in perfect rhymes.

I ne'er presume that I know best
For poetry, except my own.
I'll pen my verse, and leave the rest
To etch their thoughts in sand or stone.

True peace for man is hard to find,
And wise is one who holds it tight.
I see the truth through clearer mind,
Without the gold that hinders sight.

## Lost And Found

I

Alas! the Gates of Solitude
Extend beyond my straining reach.
Descending Hope and attitude
Inhume emotions I beseech.

The path I tread has worn away
And clouds my quest with churning dust;
So life is stripped, then painted grey,
Whilst memories are stained with rust.

Uncertainty is all I know,
And all that can be counted on,
As winds of change forever blow
To whisk me from a brighter dawn.

Encircled by expectant friends,
Depended on by family,
I pray the Lord this journey ends
Ere darkling robes envelop me.

I peer into a moiling mist
In search of Quiet's gleaming bars,
But names not etched upon its list
Shan't see the gate amidst the stars.

A precious few inherit keys
To turn the locks and enter in:
They wade into absolving seas
To purify their mortal sin.

## II

I feel, in warmth, their newfound Joy,
Like sunshine through a hurricane.
I'm once again my father's boy,
Who played in summer's crystal rain.

As Innocence returns to me,
Along with my infectious laugh,
I alter routes and move alee,
With Faith, my sturdy walking staff.

The Tempest, chased by Hope's return,
Departs and storms my mind no more.
Through lifting fog my eyes discern
The shining grill of Heaven's door.

The lambent glow of Paradise
Cascades its light upon my face,
This weary Knight of Sacrifice,
Delivered from a dark disgrace.

With silken voice, an angel sings
Uplifting songs in flowing rhymes.
No elegies of dying kings
But words of Love in tragic times.

Though burdens sit, still on my back,
I know the Father's master plan.
I'll fight my demons in the Black,
Emerging as a better man.

# Armored In Isolation

As tattered night surrenders to the morning
Amidst a bruised and beaten sky,
The hazy heavens weep their misty warning
Of love's intent to pass me by.
The rain, symbolic of my sorrow,
Defeats today and steals tomorrow.

Unyielding dreams assault my weary mind
With visions of my deep regret;
I'd reached accord but never had I signed
My name to play, though boards were set.
I left the game of love intact,
Unmarked by honor, which I lacked.

I'm stuck in muddy grooves of flaws unbroken,
Made by the tracks of fear's machine.
I'm choking on the chunks of words unspoken
Allowing silence to demean.
So, safe in armored isolation,
I sink inside my devastation.

The Sculptress Of Slumber

Aloft I soar, bereft of wings,
But only with my lady near.
Her puppet? No, I have no strings,
But yes, her voice does bend my ear.
I know not where my dreams may steer,
But listen for the windswept rush
Of that fey tone, so sweet and clear,
That whispers through the drowsy hush,
As waking Dawn prepares a hue-tipped brush.

She takes the clay of wayward dreams
And molds it in her magic way.
Amidst the soft Elysian beams,
My nightmares melt beneath her sway.
As darkness lifts, replaced by grey,
Another night is near its end;
But eyes will greet a sparkling day
That glides upon a summer wind,
Enchanted by the light my dreams portend.

The Fortress

Past dew-brushed fields of gleaming grass
Where dawn's arrival battles gloom,
There lies a wasteland's bitter mass
Within a cloak of mortared doom.

From bleak stone base to metal sky,
A fortress looms in starless night;
Its watchers gaze from tower high,
The turret scarred by ancient fight.

Once proud and tall beneath the blue,
Now shaded dark in solitude,
Its gates were sealed as anger grew,
And friendship's touch was misconstrued.

Here dwells a lord of twisted realm,
Who writhes inside a fractured mind;
A king of fools, his crown a helm,
His weary visage deeply lined.

Inside the stronghold forged by fears,
The exile shuns all human touch.
His crinkled eyes are mapped with tears,
This crippled man without a crutch.

He looks upon a queenly throne,
Illumed by flame from candle glow.
His spirit falls through flesh and bone,
As dreams of love no longer flow.

The decades scroll on castle walls,
Untouched by siege or war within.
The echoes fade down empty halls
Like beating hearts when slain by sin.

With silent steps one winter morn,
A maiden comes, adorned in white.
She melts the frost with warmth reborn,
And fills the dale with beauty's light.

She nears the gates, her eyes ablaze,
And, by her voice, the chains untwine.
The fortress breathes in yellow rays,
And color coats the tarnished shrine.

She enters in with fragrant scent,
And sprinkles dust about the place;
The fortress glows with steely glint,
And wreaths in gold her royal face.

The time-torn king had found his queen
To always rule this verdant land.
A palace rose in silver sheen,
And ground the fortress down to sand.

I slip from sleep to end my dream,
And brush away the tousled strands.
A cruel mirage, this joyful theme,
For 'round my room the fortress stands.

## Lorraine R. Sautner

Lorraine R. Sautner is a lifelong New England resident living in Danbury, Connecticut. She is a 1989 graduate of Western Connecticut State University with a B.A. in English and will graduate in 2005 with a Master's Degree in Information and Library Science from the Pratt Institute in New York City.

Lorraine likes to write both structured and free-verse poetry and enjoys exploring romantic, spiritual and transcendental themes in her writings. She hopes to use her poetry as a vehicle for sharing her Christian faith, as well as the hope, love and security available to all who ask and believe.

She would like to thank her friends at Emerging Poets and TJMF Publishing; her kindred spirits David Bradsher and Dave Caudill for their support and inspiration; her parents, Bill and Regina Sautner; her twin brother and sister-in-law, Will and Erika Sautner; and her loving friends, especially Christine, Bob and Joanna Lombardi, Nescher Pyscher, Pete Howland, and little Maddie. Most of all, she would like to thank God, through Whom all things are possible.

# Gift From The Sea

Reclining in languored serenity
upon midnight's shifting sands,
a brackish breeze caresses my face,
unpins my hair into wanton wisps.
Amber rings from luminous fairy moon
whisper silvered secrets upon the surf,
roll their enchantment between the waves.

Bathed in sea mist, my spirit reels
as pounding surf crashes, retreats
slowly working its tidal magic as I inhale,
exhale in unison with moonlit ebb and flow.
My heart in dreamy staccato beats
against the tide, surging as I emerge
from frothy deluge
mesmerized, transformed:

A mermaid queen shimmering,
regal with iridescent authority.

Sovereign over all that swims,
commanding all that dives or surfs
or breaches,
I rule with benevolent supremacy
those feminine deep-water mysteries
which harness the sea's restless power
and mark its volatile currencies.
No manmade finery could
enhance my naked splendor;
no bejeweled coronet could
outshine my glorious tresses.
Starlight is my only adornment,
passion, my only crown.

What if on tide's fervent breeze
I traveled, across sanded riff
venturing far from ocean's shore
to love's southern domain?
When upon his sleeping form
I did draw near, would he awaken?
If upon dreaming lips I whispered,
bestowed a lingering kiss, would he respond
to caress of tendrils damp upon his neck,
to part the night and taste my salted desire?

Sighing, would he shift from landlocked mooring
dive headfirst into the heart of my reverie,
plumb the depths of longing
to find the rhythm of our sea?
My merman king
worshipping until we sleep sated
upon love's golden beach,
anointed only by the tender tides of time?

As I lay dreaming
upon midnight's shifting sands,
the sea mist stirs, extends
a waking hand upon my furrowed brow,
and fairy moon gathers her starry blankets.
Noble king and queen bow, retreat
into their nocturnal seaside kingdom,
as daybreak stirs from fitful, restless
slumber.

Silver Blessings

What is a shimmer across the night sky
but the fade of twinkling grace,
a celestial memory
of silvered imprint trailing:
The shooting star for which all evenings wait
...rendered more poignant
by its fragile and transient beauty.

What is a prayer
but a spoken aria,
a tender heartsong murmured
sotto voce. A whispered healing
soared in crescendo of crystal intention,
floating...sparkling
into violet librettos of time.

What is a whimper
but night tears singing
in sorrowed isolation,
fear keening on a crumbling ledge
of hope...a silent invocation
to the Alchemist of Love.

Who then is a friend
but one who sees,
hears the brilliance of a soul still veiled
in midnight...sifts the silence
for golden truths unspoken.

A sterling nightingale heralds the light
long before the dawn,
warbling showers of silver blessings
upon a friend, in faith believing
in the heart's illumination.

Such is the poet's gift.

Prelude To A Kiss

Oh, your welcome voice
which streams - all lilac boughs
of dreams deferred, heavy
curled and whispered
in moist waiting.
~

Speak, my Love,
in slumbered silence -
Arouse the soft and petaled void
into small
beaded promises
of tender encircling;
What jeweled unfolding!
~

Yes, sweet Breath,
drape me in a violet crown
of murmured vows -
Adorn this eternal blossoming,
Ascend!
~

Beloved
song of many dawns,
a Prelude begins
which will never cease
from beginning.
See, our kiss has already started!
...in words
whose fragrant origin
never ends.

Good-Bye

I keep
reaching
over words unspoken,
beyond love interrupted.

My heart never stopped singing
in dazzling displays
of lavender vibrato -
all giddy, iridescent wishes
never quite abandoned.

It's never
too late for a wave
of sweetness
to overtake, for daydreams
of flame
still to blossom.
It's never too late
to say

good-bye.

## The Prayer

I said a prayer for you tonight.
And doing so, released into obscurity
a fragile plea, a tiny pinpoint of grace
however small, fashioned tenuously
and set afloat in gossamer song...

...heard only by those pure of heart
whose destination we could only imagine
as we watched their ships
launch from our shore
and whispered to ourselves, Farewell,

...knowing we would meet again
in celestial time,
in a place whose beauty
would only break our hearts
if we could see it now.

I said a prayer for you tonight.
And doing so, sent into the breach
a desideratum, a timid firefly of hope
whose twinkling light
at first seemed pale, hesitant
as he ventured forth into uncertainty
from tarnished origin...

...yet gaining speed
and brilliance, he found his
natural medium, soaring
tradewinds infused with divinity,
joining his brethren in a borealis
of supplication, a waltz designed
to move the Heart of God.

Yes, I said a prayer for you tonight,
in fervent tone with earnest wish
to reach you, however far away
you sit, in whatever words
you use to beg release from sorrow -
I will speak them, with you.

My heart is a stalwart butterfly
clinging stubbornly to faith,
in solace as you brave your tempest,
together as we entreat the Son.

## The Seashell Of Venice

I shall not forget your song,
the stunning way
you smiled, in languid waves
which kissed
my hidden shoals
and splashed upon my shore.
~

I had
always danced alone -
no footprints
waltzed in sterling sands;
I never knew
Venetian tides could cradle
seashells under psalms,
yet whisper words
of Love
inside my
heart.

Two Hearts, One Prayer

Two hearts that dwell on distant shores
Now pray enjoined in timeless tide;
With steadfast faith, their murmured sighs
Forge Bridge of Hope 'cross vast divide.

From East and West, their pleas arise
O'er swirling doubts and troubled sea;
On gleaming steps through violet sky,
Their words ascend by Love's decree.

Imploring souls beseeching Grace
Are blessed, as God leans nigh to hear
Empassioned pleadings for a friend:
"Please Lord, release him from all fear."

"If we could, we'd take his pain
And carry it, as if our own,
Up stairs of light upon our knees
And leave it, gently, at Your throne."

In His wisdom, the Lord designs
A plan for those who long to share
The sorrowed burdens of a friend,
Which lighten, lifted up in prayer.

...Two hearts that dwell on distant shores
Still live quite far by land or sea,
But prayer has spanned both space and time
To bind three hearts in loyalty.

For David

70

Homeward Bound

When my life on earth
has waned,
When my twinkling beam
flickers, fades
from radiant helios to
modest glow -
Know my light is not my own,
Nor has it ever been.

I AM
but a fractal fire,
a brief and dancing spark
of love ~ from One
whose prismed heart
still burns.
So mourn me not.

I AM
every day that dawns.
No sunset falls,
nor fear recedes
without sweet memory
of me.

Selah.

When my journey here
is done, Rejoice ~
Knowing as I fade,
I join
exquisite Light
from which
I came.

I am homeward bound.

Sweet Leilani

Leilani
Sweet island flower,
Song of tranquility, serenade of the sands.
White ginger blossoms
Sing and sway -
Here is happiness
O Jewel of the ocean breeze,
Melody of Manakoora.
~

Dream and drift
Tiny queen of moonlight shadows.
Bathe in turquoise tides
of Paradise;
Call the setting sun.
Little heaven of the seven seas,
Salute the four winds ~
Rule the night sky.
Wish, Leilani.
Sigh
Beneath your magic lei of stars.

## Before I Go

Before I go,
before my heart retreats, turns
from dappled warmth
of autumn solace,
from sheltered sighs
of twilight memories
we discovered –

I need to touch you,
memorize your wonder
one last time.

Oh, we sang,
did we not?
Midnight songs -
harmonies spinning
into fringes of night,
the music of the spheres
whirling around us...

...as if no one before,
or since, could understand
the tremulous beauty
of secrets tearfully confessed,
tenderly forgiven.

Before we part,
before my sorrowed soul
withdraws, trailing
in its wounded wake
my damaged dreams, dismissed -
I want to seize you,
breathe your purifying flame...

Before I go,
I want to love you - fiercely
one last time.

# Winter's Healing Magic

Now is the time when lovers start to dream
Effervescent hopes in a wonderland of promise,
Snowy kisses swirling in a frozen crystal stream,
Christmas in New England has a cozy winter theme.

Heralding the New Year still snuggled in your arms,
Every moment precious in our world of new beginnings,
Reflections from the fairy lights adorning neighboring farms
Awaken feelings heightened by your playful Southern charms.

Kindling sparks and hisses from the fire in the grate,
Another moment stolen from the hourglass of heaven,
Nestled in our blanket kingdom, pondering our fate,
Poetry sustains us, makes the distance worth the wait.

Your journey has been rocky and it fills your prose with pain,
Scarred and wounded people tried to break your heart forever.
Christ the Lord has saved you and His love has kept you sane,
Healing sings on angel wings, in mending words of sweet refrain.

Every day of every week, as months roll into blissful years,
Recalling loses all its sorrows, restoring hope to your tomorrows.
In hidden ways God works His magic, evaporating pools of tears,
Lightly touching broken places, gently casting out your fears.

Outside the window, ice is coating panes with arctic frost,
Visions of enchanted shadows yielding now to morning's light.
Enveloped in our sanctuary, grateful that our paths have crossed,
Your future here is warmly welcomed, lonely days in time are lost.

Oh Nature, teach us sweetly how to yield to your seasons,
Under God in heaven, time unveils its hidden reasons.

74

Let Evening Come

Let the light fade in depleted surrender.
Let the waves break in unrelenting dismissal.
The gloaming grants no second chances.
Our love is over. Let evening come.

I should have known love's tide would eddy.
I might have noticed your constancy shifting.
A seasoned sailor would have taken warning.
My soul is weary. Let evening come.

My faith will survive fidelity's erosion.
My heart will grieve yet another good-bye.
Sorrow sleeps but for an evening:
Tomorrow beckons. Let morning come.

The Winter Queen

Winter waltzes upon the earth,
Solstice embroidered upon her skirt,
Heaven's jewels inlay her crown;
Filigree flakes crochet her gown.

In rhinestone slippers with crystal bows,
Dancing on the swirling snows,
The Winter Queen, in grand display,
Sweeps the ground in ice ballet.

Each pristine hill and highland crest,
Shimmering in its wintry best,
Greets its muse with arctic awe,
Seeks her hand 'til springtime thaw.

Opalescent strands of pearls
Enhance her thick and lustrous curls;
Diamonds sparkle at her sleeves,
Adorn her sash of frosted leaves.

Drifting clouds of nature's lace,
Dust the land with powdered grace,
Embellish every tree and hedge,
With rime up to the water's edge.

Sunshine glittering on icy stream,
Reflects the light in mirrored dream,
Snowy kisses from Queen alight,
Blanket earth in downy white.

Swept Away (By Love)

Who among us knows
the mysteries of life,
the secrets of the deep?

Who among us knows
how a wave begins
and where forever ends?

Who among us knows
that sacred place
where endless horizon
meets the setting sun?

This, my love,
I do know:

I will be forever grateful,
I will feel forever blessed

For God has let me love you

right here
right now.

Night Blooming

In shadowed grace of silvered light,
Awash in nature's sweet perfume,
My heart, that garden of the night,
Awaits its sultry, moonlit bloom.

The whispered words of evensong,
On silky petals moist with dew,
Encourage passions, ever strong,
Awaken buds with primal cue.

A roguish breeze on terrace gate
Unlocks a threshold lushly veiled,
As blossoms, burdened by their weight,
Spill ripened secrets uncurtailed.

A lunar kiss from Hunter's Moon,
Bathes virgin soil in astral love,
As trembling stems, in floral swoon,
Surrender to the bliss above.

As virile gusts from tempest dance
On tousled beds in torrid waves,
Scattered seeds from night romance
Grant fertile earth the life it craves.

The wind recedes from meadow's edge,
As daybreak drifts across the lawn,
The scent of morning 'rounds the hedge,
And flora nods in blush of dawn.

Each lustrous leaf and tender shoot
Exalts as seedlings start to grow;
Creation cradles tender fruit
And rests in blooming's afterglow.

Dance Of The Seven Veils

Memories swirl like Scheherazade
shimmering in the distance,
a verdant oasis beckoning the weary traveler
with promised relief, like a lascivious bather
plotting seduction as perfumed water
trickles down her spine
into arid desert earth.

The moon was low and full, I recall -
A million pinpoints of desire glittering
like diamond kisses against a dusky silk veil,
pinned by the ardent advances
of the Archer's deft arrow.

And all around, the heady scent of jasmine.

Flickering ash falling
red orange red in the darkness,
hot confusions of sand caressing my neck
like salacious whispers through filmy layers
of veiled modesty, abandoned at the threshold
of your canopied resplendence,
your sheltering attention.

As from a dream surprised, I awoke.
No perfumed reverie nor bejeweled chimera
had prepared my heart, awestruck in its youth,
for the treasures of Topkapi, radiant
in transported elegance, dazzling
in lambent candlelight.

It was your laughter
which broke my wonder's trance,
and seeing you my soul died
then leapt in exaltation, in recognition -
a thousand roses blooming,
a thousand words splintering
into a rainbow mosaic of unspoken secrets
for my lord most benevolent,
my Sheik.

The steady beating of the dumbeks
the reverberations of the dholki,
harkened childhood lessons remembered,
adolescent steps practiced in moonlight,
all surrendering now into
my marriage dance
for you.

The reedy yearning of the flutes
and tambourine's rhythmic clatter
seduced my hips into slow fluid motion
torso circling, arms fluttering
in graceful arabesques of praise
to Allah, the Beneficent.
And you, his faithful servant on earth.

Tempo increasing then, insistent,
universal mysteries unfurling
in the transparent rapture of my veils,
the quick staccato tapping of the zils,
Eternal feminine singing now
in the undulations of my belly,
the rolling of my breasts,
hips swaying, shimmying
in frenzied ecstasy
for you, in oblation:

I'm yours.
Seviselim!

80

Perfidy's Season

I reach for you, but garner only frost -
Your wintered soul is frozen with disdain.
The summer heat we savored has been lost,
I yearn for passion's ardor to remain.
In silence, I review the autumn past,
Recalling all the moments that we shared,
To fathom when our season's fate was cast,
I contemplate the era when you cared.
In retrospect, an image comes to mind:
You penning harvest verse in neighbor's yard.
In sorrow, I discern my trust was blind -
My next-door friend seduced my handsome bard.

With broken heart, I dream about the spring
And brand-new life the equinox may bring.

Sola Fide

Kneeling in this sainted place
of marbled grace and spired holiness,
eternity echoes, reverberates
through vaulted columns
and flickering votives of divinity -
as angels gaze with smiles
of benign, plaster
beatitude.

I relax into
all-embracing Hush
my heart exhales, my worries release
into a tangible Presence
so deep, so timeless
my very soul could surrender
to that hot stillness...

...that Peace which passes all understanding.
So calm, yet so intimate in its attending.

Never has silence spoken so clearly,
Never has stillness moved me
with such savage yearning.
I long to drink this sacred expansiveness,
taste its divine mystery:
The Alpha and the Omega
never changing, yet somehow always new.

I am only beginning to appreciate
the Heart which burns continuously
with unrequited passion;
beginning to realize
that love and sacrifice
are necessarily, irrevocably
entwined.

I am finally starting to understand
the boundless depth
of a Shepherd's fierce devotion -
To see that He can never rest,
never stop searching,
until the least of His lambs
is safe within His arms.

## Northern Lights

I can feel the magic of these chilly Autumn nights,
A symphony of promises with clarity neverending,
I behold the beauty of your brilliant Northern Lights
And lose myself in reveries of celestial love's delights.

Starlight, woo me gently with the trinkets you bestow,
Shower me with silver kisses raining down from heaven,
Dazzle me with astral visions, bathe me in your fiery glow,
Whisper to me sacred secrets of the mystic sky we know.

Lift me far from terra firma, twirl me 'round in fall's ballet,
Christen me Orion's princess, adorned in constellation's crown.
If you ask, I'll marry you and toward Elysium dance away,
Trailing nuptial stardust as it trickles, spills from my bouquet.

*"We are all lying in the gutter, but some of us are looking at the stars." - Oscar Wilde*

Bird Of Jove

When you can see beyond mourning's horizon,
When you can dream beyond yesterday's end,
You will fly, blessed among eagles,
You will soar in faith again.

When ships set sail upon the ocean,
When souls digress in paths uncharted,
Hearts can break in tempest's raging,
Hope can heal when storm's departed.

I know the Lord will keep His promise.
I know your strength, He will renew.
You'll mount up on wings like eagles,
His love supporting you.

Life's journey is never forthright,
Perfection never without travail,
If we walk with wise men, we'll be wise,
Upon my friendship, you can prevail.

For Nescher

Afternoon Darjeeling

In the fading autumn light,
she is a study in dilapidated elegance,
a vision of lavendered grandeur
kissed by spindles and spandrels,
trailed by tendrils of English ivy.
A painted lady whose gingerbread trim
and gabled roof bespeak an era
both chaste and frivolous in its demeanor.

In her youth, God was awash in the details:
laughter pealed down polished balustrades
onto shining parquet, through graceful archways
and leaded panes of multi-colored serenity,
skipping and flouncing in lemony whirls
before spilling out onto spacious porches,
swirling at her feet, settling with contentment
as she paused, carefully pouring
the Afternoon Darjeeling.

Four o'clock hailed the glint of polished sterling
on crisp white linen, a daily circus
of mismatched china and Bavarian crystal;
crumbling shortbread and scones dancing
regal upon their lacy doilies; chocolates tumbling
amongst clotted cream and fruited jams.
The heady scent of peonies languished in
the rafters, a soothing conduit
stirring the senses of souls assembled
to sip that steaming elixir,
dispensed with charm and sympathy
from the heart of a loving matron,
in conversations shared
with studied ritual.

In the fading autumn light,
she is still a study in bygone elegance,
a poignant reminder of passing days
both noble and beautiful.
A grand dame holding court
in the tattered heart of a teeming city;
A gracious hostess now offering hospitality
only to those pigeons nestled
within her sagging eaves.

Beads Of Eternity

Marking my progress between the Alpha and the Omega,
Yesterdays and tomorrows, forever is always the same.

Recounting eternal Truths, strung in fifteen decades -
Our Father, Hail Mary and Glory Be, all in soothing repetition.
Sign of the Cross initiates, welcomes the Apostles Creed.
Arranged in a circle of hope, these sweet and sacred Mysteries.
Remembering always the Joyful, the Sorrowful, and the Glorious
Years of Our Lord: One bead, one tear at a time.

# Lamentation

Dance with me
in Time, my fated squire.
In golden glen
wherein our honeyed hearts
did sweetly dwell.
On petaled paths, our scented steps
would often bide;
Until, by Fortune's fist,
vile victory
befell.

Lay with me
my knight, in gilded dreams:
In fragrant fields,
beside a splashing stream
of passion's thrall.
In morning mists, a kindled kiss
we oft exchanged;
Until, by hostile hand,
my warrior
did fall.

Sing with me
my lord, a grieving song.
In hallowed halls
within my stricken soul
your courage shines.
In rancid rain of teeming tears,
my heartache weeps;
Until, on Judgment Day,
our silken strand
entwines.

Forever Mine, Sweet Valentine

A sparkle of sunshine before you,
A shimmer of stardust behind you,
A wellspring of wonder within you,
What would I do, dear, without you?

A summer night without the moon,
A winter dawn without the sun,
Alone, my heart would surely break.
Because, my darling, you're the one.

Let me lavish you with love.
Let me linger in your life.
Make my wanting world complete:
Please, my angel, be my wife?

Marry me, my beautiful Valentine.
Please say you will.

# Contemplation

I am but a pilgrim on Life's wending path,
A traveler, not knowing where Fate's trail twists.
And like a bleating lamb on treacherous mountain pass,
My Shepherd leads me--safe--to fragrant, watered grass.

I am but a glimpse of what I long to be,
A shadowed star, half hidden in a shrouded sphere.
And like a twinkling comet's course that's just begun,
My light is but a pale semblance of the Son.

I am but a ripple in an endless sea,
A feeble wave, still swirling in a surging surf.
And like a land-locked vessel yearning to explore,
I search the heavens, knowing there is Something more.

La Belle Au Bois Dormant
" Sleeping Beauty"

Deep within the velvet night,
Swaddled in darkness
and draped in calm,
Destiny slumbers in jeweled abandon
Awaiting a lingering kiss.

In silken bower of midnight hush,
Beauty sleeps
in scented pause;
Beneath a canopy of sateen stars,
She longs for a sultan's touch.

In waking dream of moonlit spice,
The rajah strides
with princely force;
His golden robes in shadows swirl,
He carries a red, red rose.

Across her threshold of ruby veils,
With regal grace
the sultan steps,
In wonder, views his journey's gift:
Beholds her face in lunar glow.

Smitten by her lush allure,
As tendrils spill
on shoulders bare,
The mogul sighs in lover's trance,
As petals fall on milky skin.

Leaning close on bended knee,
He softly speaks
endearments sweet,
With heart awhirl and racing pulse,
Upon her lips, bestows a kiss.

Beauty wakes in rapt delight,
With languorous smile
returns his favor;
With modesty of night withdrawn,
She surrenders to first blush of dawn.

My Love Doth Flower

Countenance fair, my love doth flower
Sweeter in his devotion's reign,
Petals parched through seasons barren,
Bloom dewed in nurturing hands.
~

My heart hath ripened like a wild plum,
Its honeyed juices freely spill,
From orchard gate my bidding comes:
O taste and see, my fruit is good.
~

My garden thrives in Nature's time,
Its cycles softly tempered,
When winter frosts its secrets hide,
Summer's heat doth quicken.
~

My lover's tillage is thricely blessed,
His bounty is neverending,
In charity, hope and faith he sows,
May passion guide his reaping.

Knight Of Violet Fire

Comfort me with words of twilight falling,
Whisper solace soft upon my soul,
Crown my heart with jewels of your protection,
Guard my dreams, O knight of violet fire.

Midnight, when goodness lies in shadow,
Keepers of the flame savor repose,
The faithful, in slumber's sweet surrender,
Rely on heaven's warriors to prevail.

Valiant, you wield God's weapons burning,
Pierce the gloom with glory's pearly light,
Crushing sin, fulfilling missions sacred,
Championing the progeny of Love.

Hold me, my knight of spirit's warranting,
Shield me from evil's darkest hour,
Defend me 'til silver morning's dawning,
Love me, and keep my temple whole.

Migration

Imagine, friends, how we shall smile,
When, at last, our hearts are free -
Rejoicing in each golden mile
Across that shining ambassador.

Lingering tears will dry in time,
As we remember those we've loved
Traversing first that bridge sublime,
And now, we follow on their journey.

Setting forth toward crossing's end,
We move along that pathway gleaming,
Silvered threads through arcs suspend
Our souls from past to future dwelling.

Trekking high o'er troubled sea,
We breathe the air of heaven's gracing,
Our hopes ascend with fate's decree,
This gilded trail our prayers delivered.

Drawing near to yearning's border,
Holding close those treasured dreams,
We contemplate migration's order,
Across the breach to freedom's home.

# Tannenbaum

*

Oh
evergreen
with boughs
unchanging, grace
our hearts on Christmas
Day, illuminate this dark
December, festoon the night
with lights so gay. Hidden deep
within your branches, draped with
garlands edged in gold, indwells the
meaning of the season: The birth of Love
in days
of old.

Old Dreams, New Thanks

A kiss for luck, a backward glance
and suddenly she's on her way,
promises and sweet farewells
falling to everything she knows,
everyone she loves in that Old World:
Bicycles in rusted racks,
cobbled streets and sleepy market squares,
Masses in the old cathedral.
Forsaking all to join a new love,
her fiancé in Ameryka, her new life.
Do widzenia, good-bye.

* * *

A morning kiss, a glass of juice
and suddenly her day begins,
this 'holiday of thanks' she'll host
in her new home, for new family.
Washing carefully her wedding china
so crystal shines, silver spoons gleam
upon her grandmother's white tablecloth.
Carrots chopped, meat simmering
in a new melting pot, this old recipe
used for new traditions.
Sighing, she contemplates this day
we set aside. This new way
to love, to give thanks.

A dinner kiss, on both cheeks,
Old World charm from doting spouse,
family and friends gathered
around this bountiful table,
lush with culinary abundance.
A centerpiece of bittersweet
curves around flickering candles
as we clasp hands, form a bridge
of then and now. A prayer of thanks,
in gratitude we pray, for America:

Still the land of new beginnings.
Still the land of open arms for all.
America, which never stops welcoming
old hopes and new dreams, shared together.
In different tongues, with different faiths
we love. For blessings old,
For blessings new, we live.
We give thanks.
We give thanks.

For Joanna Iwanska Lombardi, my "little sister."

Outpouring

I am a fountain flawed
Pouring forth Your love.
Shimmering drops of mercy,
Crystalline tears of compassion
Overspill, tumble from my Foundation.

I am merely an atomizer,
A struggling conduit of Your Spirit,
Not worthy of drying the feet
Which carry me, nor the hands
Which lift me. Selah.

My heart is a cracked cistern
Drawing from Grace, yet retaining
Little from abundance offered.
If from modest reservoir I partake,
Consider truly the vastness of its Source.

Sanctum Sanctorum

Follow me.
Take my hand and we can fly.
Oblivion, never as sweet
Transcendence, never as fragile
as our holy freefall,
our esoteric shrug of surrender
into the shelter of Sanctum Sanctorum,

halfway between home and eternity.

Your question? Bring it.
I know the place where wonder is created.
Knock, and the door will open.
Ask, and you will receive, wholly.
Your bittersweet redemption
eclipsed only by the anguish
of your prolonged
confinement.

Hope with me.
Let me show you, tenderly,
how shadows are illuminated
and treachery is forgotten.
Behold, again, the brilliance of a soul
as murkiness recedes,
as despair unravels.
The human condition reversing,
trembling as it yields to the embrace
of a sacred Valhalla.

Love In Season

Late at night
I'd sit and wonder,
tea grown cold and notebook slipping
from languid fingers,
how the seasons of love would mark me,
how my soul would incorporate your appearance.

Has it only been
four months
since I would sigh when day was done?
Praising God for all His blessings
yet suffering still
in some interior way.
Silent as I courted slumber,
tears mixed with smoke
from a solitary bedside candle

light gone, but loneliness never quite
extinguished.

Changes now, small on the horizon.
You stand patient
at Destiny's door,
eager to explore the remotest corners
of my devotion, without a map.
Trusting your God to guide you;
Trusting me with the vulnerability
shining in your eyes,
with the brilliance of your intuition.

Even now
as embers burn
steady in my heart, I am afraid.
Fearful to believe, to trust
in the security of your affection,
in the promise of barrenness
finally over.
Tell me again how it will be:

How poets scatter words
and lovers gather dreams together.
Whisper again our secret plans,
and I will sing to you of
Love in season.

## Warrior's Haven

Let my arms be for you a shelter,
A haven safe from living's battle,
A stronghold in the heart of darkness,
A sanctuary for your soul.

Upon my knee, lay your weary head.
Confide in me woes from combat's raging,
My heart o'erflows with solace holy,
My kiss, a tender emissary of Love's restoring.

I yearn to hide you in the sanctum of my devotion,
I long to keep you in the embrace of my forever,
But hatred's warfare is never ending,
And you, a steely warrior in faith's most noble quest.

Come to me, my beloved soldier,
Lay down in safety through evening wondered,
Your home my spirit's gift indwelling,
You'll leave when morning's song is sung.

In The World, Not Of It

I am a silvered thread that dances
from fore to aft in one of France's
Bâteaux-Mouches, a phantom ferry,
waltzing toward Gallic estuary
of the River Seine, at midnight.

Adorned with memories and moonlit kisses,
collecting dreams of Parisian misses,
my starboard lights are coyly winking
as broken hearts I keep from sinking
off the Pont des Arts, the Lover's Bridge.

In the night, when all are sleeping,
a romantic vigil I am keeping,
patrolling close these sacred waters,
gathering forsaken hopes of daughters
whose lovers have left them...quite dejected.

In the world, but not quite of it,
my raison d'être is divinely lit
by Sacré Coeur, whose redeeming pain
as I journey toward Alsace-Lorraine,
leaves shattered promises healed, and long forgotten.

## Friendship's Garden

For reasons of His own devising,
In accordance with His vision true,
God did not give me a sister,
But out of love, He sent me you.

By what standard can I compare,
The pleasure of a thousand smiles.
Your loyalty and fierce devotion
Through adversity and thorny trials.

When I think back, I have to laugh
At all our antics back in college,
How boyfriends and our social lives
Eclipsed our so-called search for knowledge.

Through the years, how we have grown
Yet still retain that sense of wonder -
A lively joy in life mundane,
No hardship or concern puts under.

I think perhaps you said it best,
In your own words of lovely prose,
And through your illustrations of
How through seasons friendship grows:

"A friend is like a springtime garden,
A symphony of purple, red and blush,
A diamond light in dark of winter,
A forest cool in summer's crush.

She's an elaborate moment in time
When love and comfort are always near,
A delicate whisper from the sea
Soothing hearts and lessening fear.

Think of her as life goes by,
Love's timbre maturing as life defines
Separate journeys you'll travel together.
In faithful spirit, how she shines!"

*For Christine Maria Lombardi with love.*

The Alchemist

If accountancy were a dark art,
he'd be a High Priest,
cloaked in deductible
interest income, conjuring
diabolical formulas of amortization,
and whispering incantations
in praise of the unholy
power of compound
interest.

"Abracadabra," he whispers
smugly from within the
walls of his Enchanted
cubicle. "For lack of verification
nations have crumbled and
rulers have fallen upon their
swords."

Sighing heavily, he
closes his eyes, feeling
acutely the burden of his
legerdemain, his exacting Craft.
"Fools!" he hisses, incensed.
"They heed not my prophesies!
Each goes his own way,
seduced by illusion."

Staring intently,
he stabs at computer keys
in a frenzy of numerical
alchemy and a trance of
long-division.

"It is finished," he sighs
dramatically, resting his head
on his fingertips. "I have exorcised
the demons, conquered the spirit
of inaccuracy. The realm is safe
once again."

In a state of near exhaustion
and with trembling digits, he
raises to the heavens
his financial masterpiece,
lit from within by a supernatural
actuarial luminescence.
And in a final gesture of renunciation,
gently surrenders it to his Outbox.

...the expense reports are now complete.

A Sock's Lament

Has anyone ever asked
the soiled sock
how it feels to journey?
To walk a thousand miles
in someone else's shoe,
bearing the taxing weight
and heavy burdens
of another
without complaint,
Marching always to the beat
of someone else's drummer,
yet asking for nothing in return?

Fulfilling his mission
humbly, silently
he takes the high road
or the low road as he is bidden,
bending his will,
the very heel of his being
to the sole of another,
however unpredictable
however imprudent.
Feeling exhausted and soiled
his only reward, does anyone
ever say, Thank You?
Well done, my good
and faithful servant?

Has anyone ever asked
the soiled sock
how it feels to be redeemed?
To plunge gloriously
into steaming ablution,
soapy elixir pulsating,
cleaning from the inside
all that is stained and tainted
from without?
Feeling again that hot release
from past missteps,
savoring renewed ecstasy
in being made pristine...

...yet knowing he must soon begin his journey again?

## Dressed In Moonlight

I would come to you in evening,
My love alight, tremulous
Under midnight's carousel of stars.
Eager, in alabaster innocence,
To sip the cup of passion's longing -
to stand before you
Dressed only in a moonbeam's
Shimmering caress.

## David Lee Caudill

David Lee Caudill is a resident of Dayton, Ohio and discovered poetry through songwriting. Poetry became his means of escaping from the reality of everyday life in order to release feelings that otherwise remained sequestered, helping him to nurture wounds from tragedies experienced.

David became a Loan Coordinator for National City Mortgage shortly after attending Thomas More College in Crestview Hills, Kentucky. His influences for poetry are Edgar Allan Poe, Alfred Lord Tennyson, and the co-authors of this book.

He first and foremost would like to thank God, for without Him he would not be here today. He would also like to thank everyone at Emerging Poets, Lorraine Sautner, David Bradsher, and Charles Bradsher for their influence on his poetry and his life. He would also like to thank his mother Vanessa, his brother Derek, and every family member and friend who has been there for him since the beginning.

Lastly, David would like to dedicate this book to the memory of his loving father Dave, who is greatly missed by everyone who knew him. "Your tears fall as rain from the sky, joining mine as they cover the ground below. If I could wish upon a Heavenly star, I would wish to hold you again just as my tears hold yours."

To M. -

Her eyes explored the starlit sky,
Awaiting words from his goodbye,
But silence sung a nightly tune
Upon the ears of Crescent Moon;
'Tis wonted by the month of June
In which he graced her doting side,
His ardent and his faithful bride.

Alas! She sings her mourning song,
To seraphs 'mongst the Heaven's throng,
With yearning for the past to be
As one with her; she cries to thee
To acquiesce this earnest plea:
A whisper of the word "goodbye"
From Heaven's starry ebon sky.

Whilst weeping 'neath her widowed veil,
Her clamor speaks to no avail.
Though time attempts to be a cure,
Bereavement she must now endure
As answers thus remain obscure.
This anguish rests upon her brow;
If only they could speak somehow...

But spirits dwell within the soul
Of those whose mem'ries we extol.
As silence sings its nightly tune,
She sees the smile of Crescent Moon;
A sign of reuniting soon
For love's eternal waters flow
Into her heart like long ago.

114

Eternal Slumber Of The Angels

Years ago, 'midst mourning fears and fictile roses,
The tears flowed like rain – with rain – upon burrowed soil.
Veils were lowered as sanguine eyes sought refuge;
Brows were lowered as thou descended'st into Earth;
Sorrow rose as Fate attained its throne.
(Or was it Sorrow that attained this dictatorship?)
'Twas thy mother and I that wept upon thy crib;
Not for the moment that rested upon us,
But thy verdict of eternal slumber that Fate ruled upon.

My hands rested upon the chill of thy pall;
The chill rested upon my heart that descended with you.
'Tis not I who must judge "Why?"
(Oh, why must thou leave me now, with no goodbye?)
But 'tis I who must discern "Why?"
(Such an answer rests many moons from now, if at all.)

Dearly beloved – dearly departed – we've gathered
As roses upon thy bed, weeping petals of love
That shall only bloom for Mind's eye from this day forth.
Tho' darkness resides within the realm of your existence,
Thy light shall reach through the emerald blades,
Caressing the memories thou hast ne'er created –
Caressing the memories thou gave'st to me –
Remembering the caresses thou gave to me.
My heart ascended with you – into the diamond sky –
Thy smile prospers with you – upon Crescent Moon
That Heaven lends thee – for Love yields a verdict
Of eternal slumber for thine Angel.

Valley Of Forgotten Souls

By father's grave I often kneel,
My painful tears I can't conceal.
While gazing over rows of stone,
I realize I'm all alone.
Each headstone holds a plastic rose
That dances in the summer breeze.
Beyond the shadows, sunlight glows
Through rustling leaves of old oak trees.
Though peaceful views this valley yields,
Forgotten souls roam lonesome fields.

They're laid to rest by loved one's tears,
Yet visits wane throughout the years.
While guests are few and far between,
The souls' new home remains serene.
As seasons change and fall draws nigh,
The leaves lay softly on the ground.
That summer breeze has said goodbye,
The valley's left without a sound.
Again I kneel at father's bed,
Alone once more amongst the dead.

The grass has grown its final blade
To cover soil where dad was laid.
His soul a part of Heaven's plan,
Returned to dust where he began.
As winter's chill has settled in,
The leaves take shelter under snow.
No flowers dancing in the wind,
The ice sets shiny stones aglow.
No footprints seen amongst the rows,
I kneel alone as sorrow grows.

Though time has tried to heal the pain,
My tears of sorrow still remain.
This valley is my place to mourn,
A path to father's grave I've worn.
The flowers born of every spring
Surround the trunks of every oak.
As newborn Robins learn to sing,
They warm my heart that's long been broke.
I kneel to say a solemn prayer,
May each forgotten soul God spare.

## Magnanimity

Afflatus depths demise with time,
As days ahead yield mournful grief.
From darkened holes of loss we climb,
While siblings fight through disbelief.

Myself, I wane from helping hands,
While feeling falseness in their aid.
Entombed by time's incessant sands;
By death, I live through life betrayed.

In search of one's divine avail,
I turn to those of elder age.
My brother's far too young and frail,
Incapable of love's engage.

Yet as I sift through thoughts within,
Requested guides elude my call.
My sibling soothes me with a grin,
His courage standing proud and tall.

With innocence he gives his heart,
Unknowing of the pain I bear.
Benevolence, his given art,
Unbuilds the walls of my despair.

Through him I find angelic light,
As sands of time he parts with grace.
Unyielding to remorse's plight,
He heals me with his warm embrace.

Magnanimous is brother's soul,
For age holds not the telling tale.
This child I hold has made me whole,
Our sibling bond shall never fail.

# The Call

I wander down this Earthly trail,
Awaiting Heaven to prevail
From His return; but no one sees
How sickness spreads by doubt's disease
And non-believing man's reprise.
Confusion reigns within my mind
While seeking help from those left blind
By dismal souls who've left behind
The spoken word for all mankind.
A single task – though tough indeed –
Is left within my shaking hands:
To prophesize His righteous creed
Without the use of strong demands.
I question why 't is left to me
To be the voice of His decree?
I cannot be the strongest man
To oversee His pious plan!
But questions come as pouring rain
With answers I cannot retain,
For Heaven's plan remains unknown
'Til those now blind are left alone.

She Lies...

She lies...
among feathers entombed
by cotton cases, gracing
her innocent smile as she sleeps.
Her naked gooseflesh reaches
out to me, needing my warmth
to return her fluent skin to its
gentle state.

She lies...
whispering faint words as
the raindrops outside awaken
her mind. Her eyes remain
softly closed, seduced by
lucid dreams as she rests. Her
hands reach for me as I
embrace her.

I lie...
soothing her with my warmth.
I feel her heart beat increase
as I comb her hair with my
fingers, whispering in her
somnolent ears how much I...
Love her. Slumber greets me
as the words falter from my tongue.

I wake...
My arms still embracing the
wraith of her. Cotton cases
indented by her beauty
that once was...
here with me. But she lies.
Tonight. Somewhere far away...

## The Seraphim

I pace the paths of wooded fields
Where whisp'ring winds bring life to dreams.
The sun behind the timber shields
Casts shadows o'er the flowing streams.

The Robins sing alluring tunes
And bask in placid domiciles,
While butterflies escape cocoons
And learn to fly in dainty styles.

Ahead, the rolling hills collide,
Exuding views of fantasies.
The flowers blooming side by side
Are dancing softly with the breeze.

I pause a while to sway in time
With rapids from the fluent brook.
These new euphoric visions climb
And steal my breath with ev'ry look.

Beyond the brook and birds and trees,
A soothing voice concedes my bliss.
I hearken words it speaks with ease
To lure me to the hill's abyss.

Though hesitant to venture on,
I tread the path toward the call.
My inhibitions dead and gone,
I migrate from the forest's wall.

I fast approach the hillside cave,
Engulfed in sun's horizon flame.
The darkness cools this Earthly grave
And traps me in its shadowed frame.

As silence speaks to raise my fear,
A vapored mist bedews my face.
While inhibitions reappear,
My limbs create a self-embrace.

Again the voice I hear with haste:
"Come unto me," its beckoned call.
This seraph voice appears misplaced
Within this evil darkened hall.

Contrite, I trail this faceless man,
Still blinded by the cavern's murk.
Our hands convene to heed his plan
Of journeys I would choose to shirk.

Yet still I play the pantomime,
Abiding by his strong demand.
Into the dark abyss we climb,
Encountering uncharted land.

Ahead, a flame illumes the cave
And stimulates the evil tomb.
I pray He'll make me strong and brave
While entering this cavern's womb.

I close my eyes, afraid to forge
Into the hellish blaze perceived.
Enkindled by the flaming gorge,
I presuppose I've been deceived.

Yet still the seraph shepherds on,
Undaunted by Abaddon's fire.
Into infernal depths we're drawn
By voices of the Hades choir.

Our journey leads us to an edge
Where darkness meets the beckoned flame.
We teeter on the cavern's ledge
To diabolical acclaim.

I reach toward the guide I trail,
Attempting to demur our leap.
My words evolve to no avail;
The seraph cooed my cogent weep.

His soothing face bestows a smile,
Reverting to the wretched flame.
A victim of the Archfiend's guile,
This fated war he shall proclaim.

I yield a final hopeful prayer
For guidance through this bitter fight.
We soar into the scorching air,
Toward the depths of evil's plight.

Where embers sail from dastard's pit,
We plummet through the chasm's soul.
From razored screams the imps emit,
My terror consummates their goal.

The molten streams of evil's bliss
Arise to greet their falling prey.
Accosted by a serpent hiss,
We crash to realms of death's decay.

Disjoined from seraph's guiding hand,
I search through torrid flames for aid.
The eyes of incubi expand
And glisten in their cutlass blade.

Besieged, I seek evasion's path,
Inflamed by coals of heinous pyre.
The loot of evil's aftermath,
I'm trapped inside this wicked fire.

Yet still I fight for cognizance
As swords are swung with reckless haste.
The demons quicken their advance;
Their victory they now foretaste.

As tremors of defeat emerge,
A curing scream foments the cave.
This sound of beauty starts to surge
As seraph rises from the grave.

Exhumed, amid the blazing hate,
The seraph parts the molten sea.
My warring demons now abate
And raise their eyes to his decree.

Though flames surround his glowing form,
They cease to burn his brilliant gown.
Ascending from the torrid storm,
He manifests a haloed crown.

As serpents hiss and imps convene,
The seraph falls toward their throng.
The incubi turn lustrous green
And wail to douse the angel's song.

Yet still the seraph wages war,
Descending to Abaddon's field.
The solo knight of Heaven's corps;
With gallantry, his faith's revealed.

The demons rush to meet his plight,
Unveiling fangs with venom rain.
Their fiendish scimitars ignite,
Defending Hades vile domain.

The seraph lands before the horde,
Undaunted by his raging foes.
While gazing at each imp and sword,
His poise to save my spirit grows.

As demons strike with reckless force,
Their swords assail the seraph's form.
They smite devoid of all remorse
And magnify their ravage storm.

The serpents bind his ev'ry limb,
As venom's freed within his veins.
The seraph's eyes becoming dim;
His body's only still remains.

But Heaven's hands, still comforting,
Now breathe new life into his soul.
Though serpents still attempt to sting,
The angel reattains control.

He walks upon the demon swarm,
Compressing fiends with ev'ry stride.
The writhing serpents now transform
To ashen dust as each one died.

The seraph reaches for my hand,
Unveiling wings of lucent gold.
Abiding by his warm command,
I grasp his hands I now behold.

We soar above Abaddon's fire,
Demolishing the cavern's dome.
To Heaven's gates we now aspire,
The final journey to our home.

We grace the clouds 'neath azure skies
As hymns are sung by seraphim.
A myriad of saints arise,
Embracng me with ev'ry limb.

I kneel before the pearly gates
And pray He'll wash away my sins.
The Kingdom's entrance now awaits
Where everlasting life begins.

I rise to greet my guardian
That saved me from Abaddon's rage.
This angel touched my burning skin
And healed me with his holy sage.

Renewed, I walk the corridor
Among the blessed deities.
My angel, brilliant as before,
Descends with honor to his knees.

As tears begin to fill his eyes,
He holds me to his sacred soul.
Beneath his cherubic disguise,
I see the man I now extol.

He raises high his wings of gold
And yields a sight of days now passed.
By Heaven's will his hands unfold;
My father's face revealed at last.

Shangri-La

Thy numbered days have reached an end
As ache becomes too much to bear.
Goodbyes, though seemingly pretend,
Are ne'er a task that we prepare.

I view thee now, as time departs,
With no return from curtained eyes.
The final beat of molded hearts
Succumbs to rest as tears arise.

Behold, thou hast escaped the hold
That perished with the final breath.
No further ailment to be told,
Just painless days upon thy death.

Thine eyes may hide the fear inside
Behind a mask of Future's reign,
But destiny's Celestial guide
Shall comfort thee in His domain.

The broken Earth provides thy trail
To opened doors of Wonderland.
Though covered earth shall end the tale,
The epilogue of peace shall stand.

For dust within thy temple turns
To golden wings on clouds above,
And though thy loss within us burns,
Thine heart still beats with endless love.

A Sonnet To My Mother

I'd lie awake and listen to you cry,
You'd gasp for breath through sobs of disbelief.
Though just one wall divided you and I,
Our distance stayed the same throughout our grief.
So many nights I wished to hold you tight,
Our prayers could join as one for pain's demise.
Yet fear was all I held across the night,
My angst kept me from comforting your cries.
Though father's death had left us both distressed,
I vow to help you through our grieving days.
To have you as my mother, I feel blessed.
No longer will I keep fear's flame ablaze.

A guiding light I long to be for you,
Please know there's nothing I won't help you through.

# The Unicorn

I've become a mere ghost amongst stone and pasture, awaiting the arrival of those once known - those once held - those always loved. See-through markers mirror my being, spawning terror inside me as I become aware of my present state. Though the garden holds many beds, I am alone - restless - the surreal territory of the real habitat reels its chains that are bound to my heart. I am once again captive of what I wish to escape; though I was once successful, my diuturnal form becomes irreversible. Time is no longer an enemy, but is still recognized as what stands between my dreams and I. A cloud hovers just below my brow, raining torrential tears that evanesce before they are visible. The ground remains dehydrated as I gaze at it through my own wraith. Tourists of the garden arrive at last as I watch them through a one-sided mirror; they're unaware they are being observed. I interrogate them with my eyes as my voice falls on still chords. For once I can reach my target. I am not succumbed to failure or shortness of desire; I can touch the ones I hold dear to my silent heart. But my touch lacks sensation as my hands pass through one of them: his clothing - his skin - his heart and soul. Tears fall from his eyes as he holds only memories of his blood. "WHY?" I scream, but no one hears me. I remain a snowflake in the glass dome, peering outside but unable to break my way through to the existence of where I long to be. I float in the wind to the mare of the crying unicorn, again trying my hand at the sensation I've longed for. Though her spiraled horn appears sharp, my hands once again lack feeling as they seek the perception of my eyes. I fall to my knees in the infinite frames of this dream, yet something... something more powerful than anything imaginable dives into the mind of the mare. She senses something near, something real yet... real. A pseudo mortal, incognito. Her hoofs reach out as if she can feel this presence - they touch my hands as she sings to the rainbow from whence she came - from whence she shall be going. We dance in the sunlight, floating across the pasture as if we walked along that rainbow, never touching the ground, though we often appear to. I cannot feel her on the outside, but I hold her close on the inside as I reach to pull her scion to us.

The sensation in my heart begins to fade -  one last effort is all that remains before they fade into the colors forever. As a tear trickles from her eye, I begin to ride off into the sunset. I breathe my final breath and whisper on a breeze that I send to her ear that I shall live forevermore, for I have realized that I am the unicorn of her eye. Her pony holds her close as his sire enters the pasture. My sire, my mare, and my brother weep for me as I wave goodbye for the final time. Once again I become the snowflake in the glass dome, floating in reverse to soar above the trees - above the clouds. Zion at last shall become my place to rest.

## My Mortal

Upon my wake, upon my sleep -
Where relics of the phantoms creep -
My heart, extinct, has skipped a beat
'Til joining the angelic fleet.
So close below the surfaced blades,
Where roots of Autumn's flower fades,
I dream of days that once were mine,
Until the sun forgot to shine;
Now just my pall and soul decline.
But mem'ries flow like fluent rain
As thoughts of thee fore'er remain;
My bride, I wish thee dormant pain
Whilst kneeling 'gainst my last domain.
I wish to spread my limbs of love
Before the song is sung above,
But doors are closed between our hearts
Where mortal rest is reigning now;
Thy loneliness resides in parts
I ne'er again shall disavow.
But lyrics of the angels' hymn
(From Heaven's song of grace and vim)
Were scored for me to rest in peace
Until the time thy days shall cease,
For visits from the love of yore
Shall live again, forevermore.

Lonely Ghosts

By wonted grief, the sun casts shadowed veils
Upon the names engraved in dateless stone.
The universe, recording olden tales,
Is singing songs where last we stood alone.
This fort, created for the lonely ghost
Who nurtures gaping wounds to no avail,
Denies my right to see its enmeshed host
Who writes upon my skin in broken Braille.
But time, the stagnant marcher of the corps,
Rejects my weeping plea to start anew.
I oft will ask myself what life is for
Without the ghost beside me I once knew.

Though answers rest on shelves below the sea,
The lonely ghosts shall live where all are free.

# Bridge Of Amour

From the depths of my soul,
Thou hast taken me back
To a place of enchantment
I so often lack -
'Tis this place of delight
I no longer shall lack.

As thine eyes all but shutter
And speak of thy heart,
I begin down the path
Thou hast bade me impart.
'Tis thy path of enchantment
I've longed to impart.

I am soothed by a smile
That adorneth thy face
And announceth thy love
By a blissful embrace -
With this rapturous kiss
I return thine embrace.

By a touch, I am flown
To Euphoria's land
That conceiveth thy flame
Thou hast wished to expand.
'Tis this flame of thine heart
Thou hast wished to expand.

As I burn from thy flame
Of this craving we share,
I'm ensconced in thine arms
As romance I declare -
An eternal and fervent
Romance I declare.

But my dreams all but cease
When I think of how far
Thou residest from me,
A romance from afar.
Yet my dreams send this wish
To a Heavenly star
That thy flame of romance
Can still burn from afar.

## Plea(Se)

A burdened path thou walkest now,
Whilst captured by a sunken bough
That holds a life's immortal need,
But tangled hearts cannot be freed
Without a soul that bears His creed.
I asked thee once, so long ago,
(My plea appearing apropos,)
To walk with me into the light,
Yet shadows reigned upon thy mind
Which spoke to thee its erring plight.
(Replies from thee were so unkind.)
Thy cogent cover never ceased,
But left thy love for me decreased
From enigmatic thoughts released;
My hope for thee was left deceased.
Our future now desists to live;
The past we never can forgive,
But light has shone upon your brow;
Thou'st realized He lives somehow!
Yet flaws of old entangle thee
And leave the shadows resting near;
Whilst prophesizing His decree,
The Earthly lusts defeat thy fear.
A burdened path thou walkest now,
For thou hast sent to Him a vow
That shall be followed through somehow.
A promise made - thy promise keep,
Lest thou shalt lose eternal sleep.

Through The Eyes Of A Child

A fragile child just eight years old,
My brother's heart was made of gold.
While holding back my tears of pain,
Our father's death I must explain.
His face adorned a joyful grin
As I kneeled down to hold him tight.
His eyes held rapture from within,
They shined of starry diamond light.
Though bliss my visit seemed to make,
His precious heart was soon to break.

He sat beside my mom and I,
Our father's brothers stood nearby.
As silence fell throughout the room,
My thoughts returned to death and gloom.
His eyes could read my ache inside,
I felt them staring through my soul.
Confusion left from joy's ebbtide,
Those diamond eyes had turned to coal.
I sighed a breath of hope's dismay,
He sensed the words I soon would say.

I held his shaking hand in mine
While asking God to yield a sign.
"Our father's gone to Heaven, D,"
The only words God gave to me.
Our bodies shook from pain and fear,
His eyes an instant waterfall.
His screams were razors to my ear.
To father's death bloom we're a thrall.
Again the silence reared its head,
A sea of tears each one had shed.

As brother's tears I dried away,
His courage laid his pain allay.
He said, "Dad's in a better place,"
A symbol of God's warm embrace.
Those diamond eyes appeared again
As brother lent us all a kiss.
The pain I felt from deep within
Had sailed and drowned in grief's abyss.
As father's new life had begun,
My brother's love was my pain's sun.

Aysha

A dream of dreams - where haunted lands
Sink swiftly 'neath the peaceful sands -
Rests softly on my sullen mind;
Placidity I wish to find
For dimness breathes throughout mankind.
My trance awakens boundless bliss
That sailed as stone through life's abyss,
Yet now I see through resting eyes
The golden roads of Aysha's prize.

The paths sustain a rhythmic breeze,
(A lulling, heavenly reprise,)
Where feathered serenaders rest
Their wingless brood on Aysha's breast.
The lilies rollick 'midst the rays
Of sun upon the waterways,
While broken ripples kiss the shore;
A faithful resonating score
Of Aysha's temperate décor.
Descending leaves of ev'ry shade,
The gambols of this promenade,
Embrace each stone below that prayed
Beside a bed the roses made.
The petals grace my weary head
As Aysha sings her nature song.
This lullaby, so softly said,
Proclaims to me where I belong.

A dream of dreams - I realize
Upon the wake of slumb'ring eyes -
Rests far within my weary mind;
Placidity I cannot find
As shadows reign throughout mankind.

## In Wrinkled Hours

My memory, a stream of flowing lore,
Yields haunting tales of Admiration's end.
In wrinkled hours, I dream of days of yore
When rescued by the temporary trend.
Convening hearts would smile upon a star
That graced the sea of diamonds 'midst the sky;
The ocean's shore, though sought, remained afar
When dust became of us with our goodbye.
As rivers bleed from eyes that gaze in pain,
My ashen heart remains a kindled blaze.
I venture forth with nothing known to gain
From life that drowned when last we parted ways.

A pleasured time is gone within a blink
When chained to love that holds a weakened link.

The Beginning Of All Things To End

In recent memory, I can't recall
A single day in which a peace has dwelled
Within my heart, my soul, or in my mind.
My inner-self denies this old request.

I stand inside a hole of no escape,
Left searching for an exit or a path
That leads me to a light that shines above.
Though within sight, it lies beyond my reach.

This light then teases me with helping hands,
Pretending to reach for me down below.
Extending within inches of my grasp,
Yet still my shadowed hands find no escape.

I drown in rapids of insanity
While boxing underwater with hope's tide.
Its wave delivers blows that bring me down,
Farther away from peace that shines above.

The ebbtide of lost hope then helps me rise,
I teeter on the brink of an escape.
This temporary motion ends in shame,
Once more I find my home where shadows lurk.

A final prayer I send for helping hands,
I ask for hope to shine its light anew
And cast itself into my darkened home,
Providing me the exit that I seek.

I wish the light would give me inner-strength,
While ceasing taunts it yields from miming hands.
If only it could reach into the dark,
Then maybe I'd escape this sorrow's grasp.

Stevie Ray – A Sonnet

With grace, his fingers massaged every string,
Flowing like raindrops in a Texas flood.
Each note was caressed by his little wing,
His passion for blues reigned deep in his blood.
Through music, he gave us all pride and joy,
Living each day of his life by the drop.
His number one Strat was his only toy,
Though he walked a tightrope, he soon would stop.
His Earthly life held him with empty arms,
Testifyin' death by a mountain's price.
Now each day he plays his Heavenly charms,
Living in Riviera paradise.

Through a life without you we're left to roam,
The sky is crying as Stevie's gone home.

## Abscessed Obsessions

I gaze the plains of severed dreams,
That left behind my innocence.
While silencing incessant screams,
The voice inside remains intense.

It speaks its needs to tiny hands,
That cannot cease to heed its word.
An effigy to dark demands,
I fight, but still remain demurred.

These haunting words convulse my mind,
And vex the thoughts that fight for peace.
My skin and nails now intertwined;
With blood, I sign the voice's lease.

Misleading me to urgent needs,
It's mirth I feel with every move.
I purge my will in flaming deeds,
While dancing in its evil groove.

Each impulse pumps with rapid fire,
As nothing seems to satisfy.
Emotions drown in ailment's mire,
While mental realms intensify.

As battles rage with malady,
I search for words of counseling.
But ramparts fall as crushed debris,
And leaves my soul still suffering.

Yet still I long to mime the voice,
While standing victim to its bliss.
Though misery was not my choice,
I'm soothed by this syndromic kiss.

Vine Of Life

As life bestows the remnants of my past,
I build my fragile walls of self defense.
From visions of mistakes both frail and vast,
I curse abyssal strife at hope's expense.
With efforts to ascend from fearful murk,
I cling to shadowed sun within my reach.
Though home remains a cave where villains lurk,
A prayer for faith and pride conducts my speech.
My new euphoric dream I hold so dear,
Yet still internal fiends corrupt my soul.
This vine of life I fight as fate lies near,
By Heaven's guiding hand I'll gain control.

May days ahead be rife with solaced rest,
This incubus within I shall detest.

## Angelic Light

I woke unto a tearful stream
That left my weak heart aching.
The cries conceived from last night's dream
When dad's life God was taking.

I kneeled beside my father's bed,
His comatose eyes resting.
Though doctors said he'd soon be dead,
I prayed for Heaven's blessing.

Just then a light, Angelic Light!
Shown brightly down before me.
My father's eyes recaptured sight
And opened oh so slowly.

I fell so quickly to the floor
As father's form was raising,
To seraph light from Heaven's door
We both found ourselves gazing.

As father looked me in the eye
He said, "I'm fine, don't worry."
My starry eyes began to cry,
The tears made his face blurry.

Though soon he left with no goodbye,
His message was delivered.
My raining eyes I couldn't dry,
My body simply shivered.

This dream, a gift from dad to child
To tell me that he's alright,
Has left my heart so warm and mild
As I think of him tonight.

I know he's in a better place,
For God has let him tell me.
Accepted into Heaven's grace
Where someday I hope to be.

Bleeding Me

The child of old appears no more;
This life of mine has aged with scars.
Afraid to open future's door,
I mask my pain with sad guitars.

They weep my tears through notes sustained,
While deep inside they play my soul.
Their strings leave feelings unconstrained;
Releasing strife's my only goal.

Though chords may sound of blues or rage,
They yield my melancholy mind.
Alone, I stalk seclusion's stage
As blood and music are combined.

I pen the words that seal my fate;
This angst and mental bankruptcy.
These euphonies release the weight
And sail my thoughts on dismal's sea.

As efforts to detain my fears
Forsake my dreams of normalcy,
I lyricize the painful years
That always seem to punish me.

While friends may cease to multiply,
My music heals my bleeding heart.
I'll forge these ballads 'til I die;
Forever bound to spawning art.

## Without Thee

How dost thou see the fearful plea
That rests so secretly in me?
Whilst kneeling just within my mind,
Afraid to speak the words I find,
Dost silence leave me weak and blind?
Requesting faith in what is right,
I crave, but leave the words unsaid.
Unnerved by solitude at night,
I scrutinize myself instead.
But hope still lives, though deep within.
(Without thee, Lord, I cannot win.)

I witness to unknowing friends,
Undaunted by their timid trends
As confidence in faith I show,
Though inwardly I rarely know
The path to let my spirit grow.
My knowledge seeps through hidden fear
Of faltering and failing Him.
The crystal visions ne'er appear;
My righteous light so often dim.
But hope still lives, though deep within.
(Without thee, Lord, I cannot win.)

At dawn, I rise to thoughts of thee;
At dusk, I lie amongst debris
Of bastions that collapse inside.
Left tripping o'er my sullen pride
Whose wishes I will thus abide.
But still I fight for cognizance
Of love that dwells within thine heart.
Please free me from this self-defense
Of disallowing this new start,
For hope still lives somewhere within;
Without thee, Lord, I cannot win.

Beginnings

As our eyes melted into one
streaming gaze, our molten hearts
began to flow as one river. Our love
stood at the base of its waterfall,
growing with every drop of our hearts
that flowed over the edge above us.
As we bathe in the collected emotions
from above, we're cleansed by the purity
of what we are, not what we were. The
past is just what it is; the future is ours
to create.

The Ballad Of Lost Ardor

When will this pain of loneliness decease
        Within my mind?
Will pleasures of my past convey a peace
        For me to find?
Will longing for a love I need
Allow my heart to soon be freed,
Or will I not discover a release
        From sorrow's bind?

I wish to leave behind the thoughts of those
        That tore my soul,
Yet still my mind surrenders to the lows
        I now console.
I battle constantly with fear
That a new love will not appear.
This fight between my past and present grows
        Out of control.

I know I once held love inside that now
        I must set free,
Yet shattered dreams and lost esteem somehow
        Envelop me.
If only hope could make its way
Into my life for just one day,
This broken heart could mend and soon avow
        This answered plea.

Silent Screams

I shade a soul that once was white and pure,
Before the reign of dusk and sooty tombs.
The past, I must relive and thus endure
As fate is locked inside collapsing rooms.

My heart, encrypted by a breathless mind,
Has perished with the wraith that disappears.
Those eyes, once full of life, are rendered blind
Throughout the realms that never count the years.

I walk along the paths that once were paved
With cushioned stone to lead me to my dreams,
But nothing on this road was ever saved
And no one ever hears my silent screams.

While searching for a ground with eyes that sleep,
I fall again where last I kneeled alone.
The edge I teeter on remains as steep
As long ago; the end I must postpone.

But life remains a course of crooked turns
With rails that disappear when shadows fall.
A circle's end is always what returns;
No matter if I run, or if I crawl.

Though silent screams have lived throughout my days,
I pray their voice will gain the strength I fear
To break the chains that bind this endless phase
And keep me from this life's supreme frontier.

Somber Resplendence

Familiar thoughts embrace my heart within,
As though the words were drawn from my own mind.
We speak of overcoming ev'ry sin
And ent'ring day, for night has left us blind.
Poetic voices linked by undersong;
The depths of which embrace my tender soul.
The child within must help this man stay strong,
For age will soon erase our self-control.
Imbrued by thoughts that fight this guilty fiend,
I grasp the words that call the silent flame.
When last these minds of harmony convened,
A heart was saved; our songs remain the same.

To know a man can speak what I can't find
Shall manifest the strength I've kept confined.

The Battle Between Id And Ego

And this I pray....

This labyrinth of sympathy
  Entraps my weakened mind,
As solitude from apathy
  I wish to leave behind.
Yet fears are still inside me,
This maze I travel blindly.
Encouragement is hidden in
  A place I cannot find.

I ask for Heaven's guiding hand
  To play the leading role.
I must attempt to understand
  Why id is in control.
I lust for Earthly pleasures,
Yet still I seek God's treasures.
This war within my mind must die,
  Enlightening my soul.

As battles rage and victims fall
  To demons from within,
I pray my ego conquers all
  To lead me far from sin.
A map I seek for freedom,
To lead me to His kingdom,
Where everlasting life awaits
  The day it can begin.

Amen.

If The Dead Could Speak

I lie within the courtyard
Of this human garden's casing,
Awaiting Heaven's verdict
Of the trial I am facing.

I ponder days with loved ones
That are now just distant visions,
Left wishing for the mending
Of my childrens' old incisions.

I watch them through a window
Of this realm where I'm residing,
Their faces drenched in sorrow
From the cries their pain's providing.

I long to hold them gently
And to whisper words of wisdom,
"Your strife is not forever,
Just a temporary prism."

Yet still I lie here silent
As the jury starts debating,
Just dreaming of my children
And the tears my death's creating.

I pray for God to grant me
Someone's voice to send instructions,
"My sons, I was invited
Up for Heaven's introductions."

The judgment has been given
As I soon will rise forever,
This angel will be with you
For each journey and endeavor.

I know that you will join me
When your verdict is decided,
   Our souls will live as one,
Ne'er again to be divided.

The End Of All Things To Come

I feel the final moments of his life,
They slip away from us as death arrives.
Hours become minutes,
Minutes become seconds.
The helpless son, I kneel and cry for mercy.

As needles play the role of life support,
Pumping fluid soul into his veins,
His breath becomes distant,
His half-closed eyes glaze over.
I visually witness the end of life.

I feel his warmth within escape his pores,
His skin then freezes me as I hold him.
The monitor line still jagged,
Though not for much longer.
It's almost time for parting words from me.

I whisper in his ear, "In case you hear me,
I hear the voice of Heaven call your name."
My mother speaks through weeping:
"Your brother's up there waiting,
Say hello to those we love and miss."

The doctor calls the family to his side,
One last goodbye is all that's left to share.
The needles are removed,
His liquid soul runs dry.
He disappeared from us with one last breath.

As screams ignite the halls adorned in white,
The jagged line of old appears no more.
The doctors then console,
I just want them to leave.
There's nothing that can help me with this loss.

A white sheet is then pulled across his face,
Symbolizing death that greets him now.
As screams become silence,
I wish to go with him.
I cannot walk this Earth without him here...

## Beyond The Rainbow

Through days of loneliness, I've wished for zeal
To comfort me when smiles were led astray.
A wounded heart must find a way to heal,
Lest happiness shall once again decay.
The world, at times, seems vague and lacking bliss
That once enkindled hearts like yours and mine.
The moment that we rave of our first kiss
Will signify beginnings so divine.
I think of you when miles are in-between;
I dream of us becoming one within.
A single chance to procreate this scene
Will show you where devotion's always been.

A treasure lies beyond the rainbow's end,
But with my heart, its wealth we shall transcend.

## Night vs Day

The day expends its final breath, relinquishing what it held as life. I breathe in the air from the exhale of trees and flowers, but their blooms seem so much more beautiful than my own. Alas, I yield what was to be my final breath from the trees, but a light flickered from the sky and rode the tail of a star I had wished upon. The star contained dreams I once held. They were taken from me and thrust deep into this Cosmo that was so far away. But now, now the light points in the direction of this burning body that tries to reach the heavens. Somehow it speaks, through the moon that is smiling in the darkness, following my misery like an orphan trying to find a direction for life. My misery and the orphan travel from home to home, searching for that guiding hand to unite the two... but help seems lost in the same Cosmo that holds my dreams. What I thought my friend was simply my imagination, for the light simply mimics the darkness as though it was a comedian. So the day inhales its new life at dawn, shining its purity on the trees and the flowers that I wish to become. No worries, no Cosmos to steal my dreams, no misery to keep me from realizing my potential, no enemies to speak when risen high above me, tearing me down with their axe-words that I can no longer bear. My branches...my thorns shall protect me from the moon's mockery, for I will be able to see that he is no better than I. I just pray that I don't start a fire.

The Last Remaining Light

Where eagles soar and clouds collide,
The last remaining light plays dead.
Though it could help my sorrow hide,
It worries of itself instead.

Igniting skies of ebon shade,
The light falls short of Earth below.
While nothing keeps me from its aid,
I stand alone where shadows grow.

With ev'ry step I try to take,
The darkness follows like a child.
It curses my nocturnal wake,
While keeping painful thoughts compiled.

Immortal deeds of self defeat,
This nemesis I carry well.
Yet somehow I must be complete,
If victory in me shall dwell.

I wish to play the King within,
While forcing dark to bow to me.
I'll gain control of mortal sin,
The final step to being free.

Though future days aren't yet alight,
The last remaining hope still shines.
I seek its comfort ev'ry night,
No longer prey to dark's designs.

## Hands Of Grace

A friend in need entreats my helping hands,
For times are tough and full of discontent.
Unable to remit each day's demands,
He spirals through his arid life's descent.
Requesting coin or bread to help him through,
I give so graciously to ease his strife.
Yet debts and hunger always grow anew;
A novelistic tale throughout his life.
But friends we are, and so we shall remain;
An armored bond we've shared from long ago.
I venture forth with nothing known to gain,
Just peace of mind from kindness I bestow.

I pray his life will strengthen from my aid,
Expecting not my gifts to be repaid.

#

His supplicating turns to harsh demands,
Yet still I wish to help my troubled friend.
No longer can I satisfy commands
That cumulate to sums I can't contend.
As sources of my aid depreciate,
I cease to grant requests of his distress.
Unable to support our merging weight,
He thieves the goods of worth that I possess.
But stones will not be cast from hands of mine,
For accusations lead to self-demise.
I yield the words in stone as Heaven's sign
To rise above his oft destructive lies.

I pray my friend restores the bond that was;
Forgive him Lord, he knows not what he does.

Feeble Fable

The depths of ardency sojourn your eyes,
Though drops of love within have evanesced.
I oft sincerely sing my heart's reprise
To uninviting ears I've left oppressed.
As efforts to demur your spurning fails,
I crucify myself with endless zeal.
Your broken ring reduced to rusted nails;
They procreate the wounds I now reveal.
Yet still I fight to conquer faithless vows,
While deep inside you seek departure's course.
Your addled soul within I always rouse
And spawn the foe that drowns our loving force.

Though fervor still resides within my heart,
My future bliss will cherish this new start.

Heart Of Stone

I question why a love would bloom so deep
Beneath the blades where roots of flowers fade;
My heart becomes a stone where blood will seep
Through veins that once were tied to our cascade.
Unable to defend my aging sins,
I watch you walk away as once before.
The path where afterlife always begins
Is where I realize I wanted more.
So why should life begin in realms afar
Before a heart of stone can beat again?
My name upon the slate becomes the scar
That lives until the Earth shall meet its end.

My closing date has claimed the end with you
Before I realized what you once knew.

Angel's Wing

A distant friend lies victimized
By healthy dreams that cease to be.
His aliment list is itemized
And growing 'gainst our hopeful plea.

My brother, in poetic mind,
Is needing prayers to soon come true.
Yet tears from me is all he'll find;
I'm helpless from this distant view.

I cry to God to save his soul;
My knees are scarred by altar's rim.
This saintly friend I now extol
Is fighting as we pray for him.

Though lights of life may not be bright,
My faith in Him is strong and vast.
A cure He'll send this peaceful night
And leave this torment in his past.

I long to go and comfort thee;
I wish for more that I could do.
But silent vows to God from me
Will soon begin his life anew.

"Please hold his hand and soothe his heart,
For you can end his suffering
And give my brother his new start;
May strength adorn this angel's wing."

Father's Pride

A tiny child of only four,
I'd wait for you by our front door.
Your days at work were long and tough,
The income made was not enough.
I'd see your car roll down the street
As I would run outside to wait.
Your face drenched from factory's heat,
You lacked the strength to close the gate.
Yet still I'd reach to grasp your leg,
"Come play with me," I'd start to beg.

You'd ask to rest just for a while,
Erasing my excited smile.
Fatigue I did not understand,
Attention I'd always demand.
Inside the door you'd nearly fall
As mom would ask if you're alright.
For her assistance you would call,
This ritual a common sight.
My tiny arms still holding you,
Attention I'd always pursue.

You'd gaze into my tiny eyes,
Then wipe away my gentle cries.
Your strength would somehow find its way
Into your heart so we could play.
I'd grab my bat and run outside
To swing at every pitch you threw.
Your face alight with joy and pride,
My blissful smile would grow anew.
You'd pick me up and hold me tight,
"I love you son," you would recite.

With every day that passed us by,
Your love and pride would never die.
Though strength would fail to comfort you,
You always made time for us two.
I never understood your pride
Until it wasn't there to see.
Though now at rest, you're still my guide,
You're never just a memory.
Someday I'll stand at Heaven's door,
Just like the child I was before.

Devotion's Reverie

The seas of adoration flow,
Like burning drops of zealous brine.
Romanticism starts to show
Through mystic eyes that gaze in mine.

I see the warmth that dwells within,
Emitting rays of doting dreams.
Her subtleties conceive a grin
And raise my passion to extremes.

She holds her breath through sprightliness
As I embrace her tenderly.
We've longed for this euphoric kiss
While time evolved so patiently.

Her breath escapes to soothe my ear
While whispers stimulate my heart.
Our thund'rous pulses then adhere
To rhythms shared through days apart.

Her subtle grin becomes a smile;
A captivating view of grace.
Our love renewed with sacred style,
Seclusion's gone without a trace.

My eyes unfold to solitude;
Another dream of parody.
As tears of misery exude,
I curse this emptiness in me.

You're Not Alone

As time bereaves the years of simple lives,
We face our days entombed by silent fear.
While clutching to a hope our soul survives,
We bear our massive cross with no one near.

This solitude disrupts our faith and dreams,
Yet still we cling to hopes of future bliss.
Each night our loneliness impends extremes,
Reminding us of zeal we sorely miss.

We long to find a love to help us rise
From rapid floods of sadness and despair,
But winds deny our sails with bitter lies,
And drown us with the cross we always bear.

Yet love is not our only taunting ebb;
We fear the loss of those we hold so dear.
They fight through life's unyielding tangled web,
Reducing us to sorrow so severe.

Alas, we find ourselves in need of aid,
While family seeks our strength to conquer all.
We fight the world forlorn on this crusade,
And pray that we survive this woeful squall.

Though days ahead seem dark with vacant hope,
A light is shining near with cordial care.
Through kindred souls we'll help each other cope,
You're not alone, for friends are always there.

Sweet Baby James

Acoustic tones adorned our ears,
Enhancing bonds of kindred souls.
We rode the Copperline for years,
Ascending us from lonely holes.

The vinyl spun through endless nights,
With Carolina In My Mind.
Though mother would eclipse the lights,
Our hearts and arms remained entwined.

Through lyrics of Sweet Baby James,
I learned to shower friends with love.
The words would douse our pensive flames
And guide us to the light above.

While times were tough and full of strife,
The music ceased our woefulness.
Though Fire And Rain described dad's life,
It never made me love him less.

Now Heaven holds my father's hand,
While all alone I play this song.
Upon my knees I often land.
No longer meek; no longer strong.

But Baby James can take me back
To days when father's hands I held.
I'll kneel and hold my father's plaque;
My tears of mourning ne'er withheld.

## The Mourning After

'Tis quiet, 'mongst the sleeping throng,
Where souls await the Heaven's song.
The diamond light from ebon skies
Casts shadows o'er the weeping trees
That hide the valley's blithe disguise;
But glist'ning tears sing death's reprise.
Alone and brimmed with discontent,
Thy mem'ries thou shall e'er resent,
For sleep erased each past event.
Now thoughts of thee lie deep in tombs
Where nameless graves yield dolor blooms,
But winds begin to speak to thee
Through voices of each restless tree
That wish to satisfy thy plea.
For souls may lie in valley's bed,
But Heaven's where thy spirit's led
To rest amongst each deity
That graced the Earth, now strong and free.
Thine hands embrace in solemn prayer,
Whilst kneeling 'gainst a temple's stair,
That souls convene once taken there.
Though winds do mourn, they often bring
Such peaceful words thy sleepers sing.

## Wanderlust

'Tis my soul that weeps of thy verdict,
For wanderlust claimed thy beating heart,
Thieving thine eyes that awoke with morning
(For now they sleep as evening's sun).

Directionless, I search for thy hand
That once rested upon my shoulder.
Thy Father-to-be seized my father from me,
For thou hast claimed His call to grace.
Upon the clouds of Elysian skies,
I vision thy phantom - adorned in white,
Host to new cherubs of His brethren -
As mem'ries rest in ebbs of ebullience;
I battle to save the dying mem'ries of thee,
Yet each new dawn births memoirs of
The timeless ending that seems of yesterday.

As I once knelt upon thy bed of soil,
I kneel again - alone - in thy fresh garden.
Colonnades of my mind hold my bastion,
Yet fractures of the walls yield collapsing.
Though night rested upon thy heart long ago,
My grief breathes as a newborn of my soul.
Shadows once understood become obscured
(Were shadows of grief ever understood?)
While virtual candles burn lightless wicks.

I pray for my own soul (as I pray for thee),
With dreams of a reunion succeeding my wake.
My heart - my soul - my undying faith in thee -
Releases thy hand that once rested upon my shoulder.
I hear a whisper on the solaced breeze -
Serenity calls thee, father, and His light
Shall forever shine upon thy soul I extol.
As I relinquish the hold, journey amongst
The brethren that wait for thee, father,
And save a trace of light for thy son.
My wanderlust seeks the comfort of
Thy hand upon my shoulder once again.